I0752856

SERMONS

BY

JOHN JACKSON.

PHONOGRAPHICALLY REPORTED.

PHILADELPHIA:
T. ELLWOOD CHAPMAN.
No. 1 South Fifth Street.
1851.

SERMONS.

SERMON I.

DELIVERED AT FRIENDS' MEETING, LOMBARD STREET, BALTIMORE, ON FOURTH DAY, TENTH MONTH 27TH, 1847, DURING THE WEEK OF THE YEARLY MEETING.

"My doctrine is not mine, but His that sent me. If any man will do His will, he shall know of the doctrine whether it be of God, or whether I speak of myself."

The doctrine of Jesus Christ has ever been distinguished from the various counterfeit productions that have assumed the name of religion, by its great simplicity, by the universality of its nature, by its complete adaptation to the spiritual wants of man, and by the influence it exerts upon human conduct and character. We have cause to admire, with feelings of gratitude, the wisdom of our heavenly Father, in that he has not made his doctrine and religion depend on the fluctuations of human opinion, but has established them on the firm foundation of eternal and unchanging truth. Neither has he made us dependent one upon another for a knowledge thereof, but has condescended to be the teacher of his people himself.

When the blessed Jesus entered on his gospel mission, he had no *new* doctrine to preach, no speculative opinions of his own to promulgate, but simply to "bear witness to the truth."—Truth as it originated with its author, and which is the same in all ages. Hence he called others to do the will of God, declaring that if any man will do his will, "he shall know of the doctrine whether it be of God, or whether I speak of myself." The religion of Jesus Christ is, therefore, the same in all ages. It is not one thing in the days of Moses, and another in the days of Jesus of Nazareth.

Although Paul or Peter, Wickliffe, Luther, Calvin, or Fox, and numerous others who have sustained the character of reformers, may all have labored in their proper sphere, and fulfilled the work, that the times in which they lived demanded, yet Christianity has never changed its character. Its doctrines and obligations have not altered, but they have been, and still continue to be, revealed to all the nations and families of the earth. We are forced to this conclusion unless we admit that God is partial and unequal in his ways, and that he has favoured a portion of mankind with a knowledge of his will, and excluded all the rest of his rational family from the enjoyment of his presence, his goodness and his regard. We must believe it if we admit the doctrine that Christ is manifested in the flesh—for wherever Christ is, there the obligations of the Divine will are made known.

We do not limit the coming of Christ in the flesh, to its appearance in the person of Jesus of Nazareth. *Christ,* that divine and spiritual illumination described by the evangelist, as the "Word that was in the beginning," and by which the worlds were made, did not for the first time make its appearance when the spirit descended upon Jesus. The same word had spoken to Adam in the garden, it had reproved the first transgressor—it enabled Enoch to "walk with God"—it pointed out to Abraham the glory of the gospel day; it instructed the understanding of the prophets; spoke to Samuel in Shiloh; it was the "Rock that followed Israel." The evangelist speaks of it as the "true light, that lighteth every man that cometh into the world;" and the apostle calls it "the power of God and the wisdom of God."

It is also revealed to us; and it is just in proportion as we become the subjects of its government and influence that we become "heirs of God, and joint heirs with Christ." It is this union that makes us Christians and partakers of the Divine nature, one with Christ and God; and it is vain for us to call ourselves Christians or followers of Christ, if we have not been made possessors of his spirit; for, says the apostle, "If any man have not the spirit of Christ, he is none of his."

The teaching and guidance of this Divine power, and wisdom *Christ,* is what we call inward, immediate, and Divine revelation—a revelation that is not limited to time or confined within the narrow bounds of sects, but has "appeared unto all men teaching them to deny all ungodliness and worldly lusts, and to live soberly, righteously and godly in this present world."

We have abundant evidence that such a revelation is universal, and adapted to the wants of man in his pursuit of heaven and happiness. In the Scriptures we find a great amount of testimony showing that the men of former generations acknowledged an immediate revelation of the Divine will to man, and we profess to believe that holy men of old wrote as they were inspired by the Holy Ghost. The writings of the Scriptures are, however, chiefly confined to the history of a single nation of people; but there are, nevertheless, to be found among the records and traditions of almost every nation, traces of a belief in the existence of a Supreme Being, and of an immediate revelation of his will to mankind. Those records or traditions were ever found, so far as they go to illustrate the universality of the goodness of God, and of his dealings with man, *are of equal weight and authority with the Jewish Scriptures and ought to be so regarded.* Inspiration was not confined to the authors of the Bible, neither does it follow as a matter of course, that every thing which is found in the Bible was written by Divine inspiration. We find in the writings of many of the ancients, whose history is not contained in that book, declarations of a belief in Divine revelation, showing that it was not limited to any single class or nation, and the universal testimony of human experience in all times, proves, that God has not left himself without a witness in the souls of his accountable children.

Well, my friends, we have access to the same inspiration which has always influenced the minds of the righteous, and that too, without any human aid or instrumentality. We are not dependent upon men or books for it. We have as much evidence that the unlettered North American Indian, who has never seen the Scriptures, nor heard the gospel outwardly preached, believes in and understands Divine revelation, as certainly as did the prophets of old, or any of the Scripture writers. He speaks of the voice of the "Great Spirit" taking cognizance of his thoughts and actions, and leading him to a life of purity and holiness. It matters not whether we have ever heard the name of Jesus outwardly named, or have ever seen the Scriptures, for such is the goodness of our heavenly Father, that he has adapted his dispensations of grace to meet our spiritual wants, under all the various circumstances in which man may be placed.

In all spiritual matters, in things pertaining to salvation, this Divine illumination is our surest guide; a teacher that can never deceive us, but will, as we obey it, lead us out of all error into the knowledge of the truth. It is this that opens to man the path of duty and convicts him for transgression; while it reproves him for doing evil it blesses him for doing good.

The duties it enjoins are the same in all ages. It leads but to one point, and that is the practice of the religion of Jesus Christ. Christianity being a Divine revelation does not change; its doctrines are the same in all ages; we are as much bound to regulate our conduct by it as the men of past generations, for it remains to be its peculiar nature, to exert a blessed influence upon human conduct and practice.

Christianity owns no mysteries, it is plain and simple, easy to be understood. We must learn to distinguish between genuine Christianity and every thing of an opposite character that bears its name; we must judge it, and know it *by its fruits.* We shall find it does not consist so much in opinion and profession as in faith and practice. It does not stand in the observance of external forms, but in daily practical righteousness. Neither does it depend so much on unity of opinion as in doing the will of our Creator. It embraces every good work of benevolence, leads its possessors to "visit the fatherless and the widow in their afflictions, and keep themselves unspotted from the world."

Such was the religion taught by Jesus of Nazareth; not as something that was new, and unknown before his time, for he came not to teach any new doctrine, as is evident from his own declaration: "My doctrine is not mine, but his that sent me." When the blessed Jesus was queried of after this manner: "Master, which is the greatest commandment in the law?" he said to the inquirer, "Thou shalt love the Lord thy God, with all thy heart, and with all thy soul, and with all thy mind. This is the first and great commandment. And the second is like unto it, Thou shalt love thy neighbour as thyself. On these two commandments hang all the law and the prophets." This doctrine, therefore, was not new, it was equally as true in the days of Moses as of Jesus. These ever have been, and ever will be the unchangeable requisitions of the Divine law, and every rational being who has ever been on the stage of action, or that ever will be on the stage of action, has been under and will be under the obligation to regulate his conduct by them.

It would be utterly at variance with what we know of the character of Deity, to suppose that he would proclaim to one class of mankind such laws as, "Thou shalt love thy Creator, thou shalt love thy neighbour;" and to another class, thou shalt *hate* thy Creator, thou shalt hate thy fellow-creature.

To love God, and to love man, embraces the whole of the Christian religion. These are among the unalterable commands of Jehovah; obedience to which uniformly produces order, harmony and happiness. While on the other hand disobedience to them is followed by contention, by anarchy and confusion, and by all the evils which render existence a curse instead of a blessing. We shall find, if we investigate the subject, that happiness can only be secured by fulfilling these laws of our being, and that our failure to enjoy it is the consequence of our own rebellion.

Now we find that Jesus, our blessed example, fulfilled this law of love; both by precept and example he endeavoured to enforce it. He reproved the Jews for their conduct; he held up to their view the *perfect rule* of morality, the law of God, from which they could easily see that every opposite rule of conduct which they had learned from tradition was *imperfect* and of human origin.

"Ye have heard that it hath been said, an eye for an eye and a tooth for a tooth, but I say unto you that ye resist not evil; but whosoever shall smite thee on thy right cheek, turn to him the other also."

"Ye have heard that it hath been said, thou shalt love thy neighbour and hate thine enemy; but I say unto you, love your enemies, bless them that curse you, do good to them that hate you, and pray for them that persecute you and despitefully use you; that ye may be the children of your Father which is in heaven; for he maketh his sun to rise on the evil and on the good, and sendeth rain on the just and the unjust."

Here then are the essential duties of religion. It matters not what we profess, or however diversified may be our speculative theology, or however various the *forms* under which we may apprehend it right to worship our Maker, still we must all fulfil these commands if we answer the end of our being. But unhappily for the professing Christian church, opinions and external observances are considered of more importance to the popular theology than loving God and loving man. A religion is propagated which does not consist in the fulfilment of these higher duties, and hence it does not exert that influence on the conduct of men which Christianity is intended to produce.

And yet we see how much contention and strife there are in the world on this subject; how the visible church has become divided into sects and parties, and what a spirit of bitterness is engendered between man and his fellow. The law of love leads us to regard all men as our brethren, no matter how widely they may differ in opinion from us, or from each other, or however various the forms under which they attempt to worship the same God. It does not lead any into contention and strife, but requires us to *do* those duties of loving God and loving man, which puts an end to all sectarian bitterness. It "lays the axe at the root of the corrupt tree."

If love were the ruling principle of human conduct, all strife and controversy about religious opinions would cease; society would unite in every work of human improvement; superstition and error would vanish; truth would reign triumphantly; falsehood, violence and oppression of every kind would be unknown.

These are the views I entertain of the nature of the Christian religion, and this the influence which I believe it exerts upon human conduct and character. This is the only religion which I would recommend to us all. It is calculated to better the condition of man. It is as wisely adapted to his spiritual wants as to the regulation of his conduct. It is a religion that purifies the soul and makes it a temple for the Holy One to dwell in. It disarms death of its sting, and the grave of its victory; and while it contributes to the enjoyment of this present life, it furnishes us with a well-grounded hope, that when done with time, we shall have "a building in God, a house not made with hands, eternal in the heavens." This must be so, if the Scripture declaration is true, which says, "God is love, and they that dwell in love dwell in God, and God dwelleth in them."

This then is the path in which Christ leads his followers. Man is created in a state of perfect innocence; by making Christ his guide, he is enabled, while passing through a state of probation, to rise from this condition of negative innocence to a state of active and positive virtue—for virtue is the resistance of temptation. As Jesus resisted temptation and thereby overcame the world, so may we also overcome the world in the same manner, for we must walk by the same rule and mind the same thing. Besides this, there is no other means of salvation.

Whatever speculations may be entertained on this subject, or whatever schemes of salvation man may embrace, his deliverance from the bondage of sin can only be affected by his being made a partaker of the Christ-like nature, and that must be like the spirit of Christ ruling in him and regulating his every-day actions, filling his soul with love to God and love to his fellow-creatures.

I am aware that these views of the doctrine and religion of Christ form but little part of popular theology. They are not considered of as much importance as a belief in particular creeds and doctrines of men. The doctrine of Divine revelation is partially, if not wholly denied by those who through the prejudices of education, are looking to men and books for the knowledge of Divine things, and who presumptuously assert, that immediate revelation was confined to holy men of old, and that it ceased when the last Scripture writer laid down his pen.

Good works are lightly esteemed or viewed as of secondary importance to man's present and eternal welfare, while the religious world seem almost entirely occupied in doubtful disputations, and endless controversies about speculative opinions.

The popular religion lays but little restraint on the every day conduct of men, in fact, it tolerates many iniquitous practices. By its fruits, it is easily distinguished from "pure and undefiled religion." When, therefore, we see that the popular profession of religion does not redeem men from the indulgence of hurtful passions, does not make them Christ-like, does not lead them to love God and one another, but lends its sanction and influence to the grossest irregularities of human conduct, and even to the commission of crime, it is well for us to examine, whether if such a religion be ours we are not deceiving ourselves, and making our hope the hope of the hypocrite, which it is said shall perish. Look over professing Christendom, and let us see what kind of fruits are produced. Let us not be deceived, "God is not mocked, such as we sow, such shall we reap." Look over our own land, and let us see whether the great profession of religion which is made among us, manifesting itself by revivals, by church-going, by Sabbath-keeping, by a concern for the salvation of the heathen, and the ceremonious observance of religious forms, is likely to better our condition, and make us what we should be, considering how much we have been blessed among the families of the earth, "a people fearing God and hating covetousness."

We see that war, with all the evils and miseries that follow in its train, is encouraged in our midst; the spirit of war, which is directly the opposite of the non-resistant and peaceable spirit of Jesus, is applauded on every side. "By their fruits ye shall know them.' Christianity requires us to love our enemies—to resist not evil. But according to the popular notions of religion, the warrior may return from the field of carnage, with the sword just drawn from the bosom of his brother, with his garments dyed in blood, and his hands polluted by the commission of crime, and still he is called a follower of Him, who said, "My kingdom is not of this world, else would my servants fight."

War is a violation of the divine law, its continuance is the effect of gross moral delusion, and yet we see how it is encouraged by the professors of religion. It would seem that they do not more firmly believe in the existence of a Supreme Being, than that they believe He leads conquering armies to victory.

The name of the Sovereign of the Universe is connected with the scenes of human carnage, and his attributes of love and mercy, are supposed to sanction "Every battle of the warrior, which is with confused noise and garments rolled in blood."

Men calling themselves ministers of Christ are enlisted on either side imploring the aid of one common Father, to inspire them with strength and courage to slaughter each other. In almost every pulpit, prayers are offered up on the occasion of victories obtained in the field of carnage and blood.

Can we believe for a moment that the infinite and unchangeable God, whose holiest attributes are goodness, mercy and love, would suspend his eternal laws, and abandon his moral government, for the purpose of allowing his accountable children to kill and destroy each other? Certainly not.

I feel myself called upon to hold up to view in this plain manner, the inconsistency of our practice with our profession, when we tolerate and justify war on the one hand, and call ourselves the followers of Jesus Christ on the other. There is no truth more easy of demonstration, than that the warrior is the servant of antichrist; for it must be admitted, that the practice of war is utterly incompatible with the practice of Christianity, and whatever is incompatible with the practice of Christianity is contrary to the will of God.

There may be advocates of war in this assembly, who are almost offended at the preaching of doctrine like this. I would have them to examine the ground on which they stand, and remember that they have as good reason to be offended at the precepts and example of Jesus. We find that he reproved the Jews for their evil conduct, when he told them, "Ye have heard it hath been said by them of old time, thou shalt love thy neighbour and hate thy enemy; but I say unto you love your enemies, do good to them that hate you, and pray for them that despitefully use you and persecute you, that you may be the children of your Father who is in heaven, for he maketh his sun to shine on the good and evil, and sendeth his rain on the just and the unjust." This remains to be the doctrine of Christ; "love your enemies" is a positive Christian precept. Does the warrior regulate his conduct by this rule? If he did, the "sword would be beaten unto a ploughshare, and the spear into a pruning hook, nation would no longer lift up sword against nation, neither would men learn war any more." If he does not practice by this rule, he is the servant of antichrist.

I have no hope that wars and fightings will cease, until the benign influence of this doctrine shall dispel the delusions which envelope the minds of men, and in the same proportion that this doctrine is embraced we come to see that "God is love," and that it is only those whose conduct is regulated by the law of love, that can have fellowship with him.

It is indeed a sorrowful reflection, that war is now sustained and encouraged by many of the highest professors of the Christian religion in our land! While many of these are looking with indifference on its dreadful ravages, hastening thousands of our fellow men unprepared into eternity, the cries of the pitiless orphan, the widow and the fatherless, are protesting against these outrages on humanity, and uttering this solemn appeal, "Shall the sword devour forever?"

The doctrine of Christ leads us to visit the fatherless and the widow in their afflictions, but it never sanctioned a practice which fills the earth with mourning, lamentation and woe; and let us not forget that every one who gives encouragement to war, is implicated in the continuance of a custom which does violence continually to the laws of God, and the doctrine and practice of Jesus Christ.

So long as the sword continues to devour, the views I entertain of the doctrine of Christ, and the conviction of duty which I feel, will lead me to bear a testimony against wars and fightings, until this frail tabernacle shall go to its last resting place, and this voice be forever silenced in the stillness of death.

"Blessed are the peacemakers for they shall be called the children of God." May this number be multiplied—let them be faithful to truth and duty, and they may yet be instrumental under the divine blessing, in advancing the peaceable kingdom of Christ, and in hastening the coming of that day, when every practice of violence and wrong shall be banished from the earth forever. My faith is in the principles of Christianity. These never have sanctioned and never can saction the practice of war, or any of its kindred evils: when these principles shall govern the conduct of mankind, war and all its evils must come to an end. It is folly for any to say that Christianity sanctions war, because by the triumph of Christianity, it will be abolished and cease forever.

My young friends, I would call your attention to these doctrines of Christ. I wish to encourage you to embrace them. This is a holy cause for you to embark in, attend strictly to the convictions of truth in your own minds, this will open the path of duty, and show you a field of labour in which there is ample room for the exercise and improvement of the talents and gifts which God has committed to your care.

Let the wise counsel of one formerly have its due weight: "Remember now thy Creator in the days of thy youth, while the evil days come not, nor the years draw nigh, when thou shalt say, I have no pleasure in them."

Our happiness is intimately connected with the remembrance of our Creator. He has brought us into being for a good and noble purpose, and we should endeavour to associate the idea of his existence and presence, with all the duties and concerns of this life. I know of no reason why we should live in forgetfulness of God, but on the other hand I see much to make us better and happier by the remembrance of our Creator.

The religion of Christ is not intended to throw a gloomy aspect over the scenes and prospects of life—it inflicts no heavy burdens, but continually holds out the cheering language, "Come unto me, all ye that are weary and heavy laden, and I will give you rest; take my yoke upon you and learn of me, for I am meek and lowly of heart, and ye shall find rest to your souls; for my yoke is easy, and my burden is light."

Think not that this religion to which I now invite you, stands in the opinions or speculative theories of men. It is not the observance of outward forms and ceremonies, but it consists in having your conduct regulated by the great principles of love to God and love to man. It is not confined in its exercise to days and times, it is not limited in the performance of our devotions in churches or in meeting houses, but it is an every day work, producing the fruits of *benevolence, justice, mercy* and *love.*

Such a religion must, from the influence it has upon human conduct, and from its own nature, bless you and make you happier in time, as well as prepare you to enjoy a blessed immortality. We feel a reward in being good, and doing good, which is a foretaste of heaven on this side of the grave. Our own experience tells us, that while "the way of the transgressor is hard," the path of the just "shineth brighter and brighter unto the perfect day."

We have no need to regard the cry of "lo, here is Christ, or lo, he is there;" we have access to the same fountain of truth and inspiration, which has led the righteous of all ages, among all people. Here is a teacher always at hand, and one that can never deceive us. Its gentle whisperings are heard within, and it only requires watchfulness on our part to understand its admonitions.

With these views and convictions, I should no more think of looking to men or to books for a knowledge of the doctrines of Christ, than I should think of committing to another the keeping of my own soul. I fully believe in the testimony of the apostle James: "If any of you lack wisdom, let him ask of God, that giveth to all men liberally and upbraideth not; and it shall be given him."

This, my friends, is our great privilege, we may ask of God for wisdom to direct us in all the duties that belong to this present state, and it will be given us. Let us therefore improve it, until we all "come into the possession of that kingdom, which consists not in meats or drinks, divers washings and carnal ordinances, but in *righteousness and peace*, and joy in the Holy Spirit."

SERMON II.

DELIVERED AT FRIENDS' MEETING HOUSE, SOLEBURY, BUCKS COUNTY, PENNSYLVANIA, ON FIRST-DAY MORNING, SEVENTH MONTH 8TH, 1849.

There is a sentiment contained in a short Scripture expression, which I have felt right to bring into view on the present occasion, not because it may contain anything that is new, but because it is a truth that I apprehend all of us will be willing to subscribe to: "Righteousness exalteth a nation, but sin is a reproach to any people." And it is because I have felt a desire that we may come to enjoy the blessings of righteousness, and escape the reproach consequent upon every thing that is iniquitous, that I am led to address you.

It may be well for us individually to make an examination, that we may understand for ourselves, in what righteousness consists, that we may not be following any cunningly devised fable, or depending on our speculations and theories of religion; but having an eye to the *truth as it is in Jesus*, pursue it, and come to the enjoyment of the blessings it ever brings with it. In my view righteousness consists in, and is the effect of, our obedience to the Divine law: it is a practical and every-day work, and as we engage in it we shall know a progression from one state of experience to another, "till we all come in the unity of the faith, and of the knowledge of the Son of God, unto a perfect man, unto the measure of the stature of the fullness of Christ. That we henceforth be no more children, tossed to and fro, and carried about with every wind of doctrine by the sleight of men, and cunning craftiness, whereby they lie in weight to deceive; but speaking the truth in love, may grow up into him in all things, which is the head, even Christ."

We should not be deceived by considering that righteousness consists in a profession of religion, in a conformity to ceremonial observances, or in a belief in any opinions and doctrines, which men have framed and embodied in what are called systems of faith and worship. For if we are only depending on our belief in these things, or in the ceremonial observances which they enjoin, we may be in the same condition that the Jews were, when the blessed Jesus came among them with the message of the gospel of light and salvation, teaching them that it was not in tithing mint, anise, and cummin, and overlooking the weightier matters of the law, that they were to be accepted, but in their obedience to the laws of their Creator, in the fulfilment of the duties that were impressed upon them by the Author of their being.

He told the people of that day, when he was declaring to them the truth of his Heavenly Father, " Except your righteousness exceed the righteousness of the Scribes and Pharisees, ye shall in no case enter into the kingdom of heaven." The Scribes and Pharisees were unwilling to receive the doctrine he taught, for their ideas of religion seem not to have extended beyond the observance of their outward rituals. They presumed that the law, with its sacrifices and offerings, its priests and temple, would make the comers thereunto perfect, and they persisted in observing those things which Moses had allowed their fathers to do " *because of the hardness of their hearts*," and instead of obeying the truth that Jesus had declared unto them, they conspired together to persecute him, and finally to put him to death.

We may hold up the life and example of Jesus as being worthy of imitation—his precepts, as inculcating the " righteousness which exalteth a nation," and the doctrines which he taught for their simple and practical character, their adaptation to the wants and condition of man under all the circumstances in which he may be placed—whatever may be his situation in life—to whatever nation, kindred, tongue, or people he may belong.

The religion which Jesus came to promulgate among men, and which is purely a work of practical benevolence, and not a system of opinions or set of forms, has been applicable to man from the beginning of the world down to the present hour, and is the religion that is taught by the Creator himself to all the children of men. Christianity is nothing new. The gospel was preached to man in the beginning, when the Creator breathed into him the breath of life, and constituted him a living soul. It has been taught to Jew and Greek, Barbarian and Scythian, bond and free, all who have feared God and worked righteousness, by whatever name they may be called, have known Christ and the gospel which is the "power of God unto salvation to all them that believe."

Professing Christians have unquestionably committed an error in making Christianity consist in a belief in a certain system of opinions and doctrine, the tendency of which has been to make religion more a matter of theory than practice, of word than of deed.

It was not so with the blessed Jesus. He never made out for his disciples any written system of belief or doctrine. He insisted wholly upon practical righteousness—love and good works. When he was queried of, which was the greatest commandment, he replied to the inquirer; "The first of all the commandments is, Thou shalt love the Lord thy God with all thy heart, and with all thy soul, and with all thy mind, and with all thy strength. This is the first commandment. And the second is like, namely that, Thou shalt love thy neighbour as thyself. There is none other commandment greater than these." He summed up the whole duty of man in these few words; he showed that religion was the same thing in the days of Moses, (for he quoted the words of Moses,) as it was then; and it is the same thing now that it was in the days of Jesus of Nazareth. The principles of righteousness which are implanted in our nature by the Author of our being, are as unchangeable as God is unchangeable. These are attributes of the Infinite Mind, and are made manifest in man for the government of his conduct, and his growth in the knowledge of his Maker, the world over. Shall I say the world over? Yes; not only upon this little ball of earth that we occupy, but throughout the boundless infinite expanse of creation, wherever there is rational intelligence, the same law prevails, the same laws govern, for the same God reigns everywhere, and is present in every part of his material and spiritual universe.

How beautifully did Jesus, on many occasions, turn the attention of the people to these principles of righteousness. Love was one of them: it was the distinguishing attribute of his Father and our Father, of his God and our God.

The apostle also had so high an estimate of it, that

he declared "God is love, and they that dwell in love dwell in God, and God dwelleth in them."

Jesus, therefore, made righteousness in this particular consist in man's obedience to the Divine attribute of love. It was intended to bless him, and it invariably does bless him whenever he comes to be governed by it. It is the influence of this principle that sanctifies the social compact—renders harmonious the relations of husband and wife, parents and children, and would bind the whole family of man in one common bond of affection. Social, conjugal, paternal, and filial love, are all branches of one great stream, all are proofs of the Divinity in man, strengthening our faith in the soul's immortality.

When Jesus pointed out these great duties of man, well might he say, "There is none other commandment greater than these." He spoke of them as the commandments, divinely given to the children of Israel. The Jews were not willing to obey this Divine law written in the heart, which would have led them into the peaceful kingdom of Christ, and made them worshippers in that temple and true sanctuary which God hath pitched and not man. Thus we hear them using this language to Moses, "Speak thou to us and we will hear; but let not God speak to us lest we die." They wanted an outward law, and an outward Canaan. Forsaking the immediate teachings of the Holy One, they soon began "to hew out unto themselves cisterns that could hold no water." They made their religion consist in the observance of external rituals, and relied upon their sacrifices and their offerings to take away their sins. The prophet

Isaiah reminded them of the insufficiency of these and of the great duties inseparably connected with a life of righteousness. "To what purpose is the multitude of your sacrifices unto me, saith the Lord: I am full of the burnt offerings of rams, and the fat of fed beasts; I delight not in the blood of bullocks, or of lambs or of goats. When ye come to appear before me, who hath required this at your hands to tread my courts? Bring no more vain oblations; incense is an abomination unto me; the new moons and Sabbaths, the calling of assemblies I cannot away with. When ye spread forth your hands, I will hide mine eyes from you; yea, when ye make many prayers, I will not hear; your hands are full of blood. *Wash you, make you clean; put away the evil of your doings from before mine eyes! Cease to do evil. Learn to do well. Seek judgment, relieve the oppressed, judge the fatherless, plead for the widow.* Come now, let us reason together, saith the Lord. Though your sins be as scarlet, they shall be white as snow; though they be red like crimson, they shall be as wool." Here the requirements of the Divine law were plainly set forth—the practical duties of life were opened to their view, and if they failed to fulfil these, in vain were all their ceremonial observances, for to use the language of the apostle, "It was not possible that the blood of bulls and of goats should take away sins."

The truth is, they never were commanded to offer sacrifices. These were inventions of their own. The prophet Jeremiah is very clear upon the subject when speaking to this very people. "Thus saith the Lord of hosts, the God of Israel: Put your burnt-offerings unto your sacrifices and eat flesh. For I spake not unto your fathers, nor commanded them in the day that I brought them out of the land of Egypt, concerning burnt-offerings and sacrifices: But this thing commanded I them, saying, obey my voice, and I will be your God, and ye shall be my people; and walk ye in all the ways that I have commanded you that it may be well with you. But they hearkened not, nor inclined their ear, but walked in the counsels and in the imaginations of their evil heart, and went backward and not forward."

The prophet reproached them for their idolatry and superstition; he charged them with having done evil in the sight of the Lord in setting their abominations in the house which was called by his name, to pollute it.

Now we see when the blessed Jesus came to this people and endeavoured to show to them that religion consisted in carrying out, in the practice of life, the principles of righteousness, he was despised and rejected by them; but, nevertheless, he continued bearing his testimony to the truth until his life was sacrificed in the cause in which he was engaged. He illustrated by his example the doctrine he taught—he proved his love to God by love to man, and the only evidence we can produce of our love to God, is the extent of our love to our fellow men.

I have said this was no new doctrine. The Jews were unwilling to receive it in the days of Moses. They rejected it in the days of Jesus Christ. And now, after eighteen hundred years have rolled away, since Jesus preached it in Judea, professing Christians are but little less prepared to receive it as the rule of human conduct. This goes to show how little has been gained by subscribing to the popular creeds. It goes to show that unless religion is made an every-day work, it can be of no possible value.

If Christianity is to consist only in a belief in certain opinions, or in the observance of certain forms, it is of no more value than Mahometanism, Paganism, or any other form of worship whatever. But, my friends, it is otherwise. Christianity is intended to be a *rule of life;* it is designed to elevate man from the image of the earthly to the image of the heavenly nature; to bring him into that state of *oneness* with God, which Jesus spoke of in his beautiful prayer: "That they all may be one; as thou, Father, art in me, and I in thee, that they also may be one in us." The apostle also exhorted the Philippians, "Let this mind be in you, which was also in Christ Jesus, who, being in the form of God, thought it not robbery to be equal with God."

Are we prepared to believe the doctrine of Jesus? Are we willing to follow in his footsteps until we also come to be "heirs of God, and joint-heirs with Christ."

I look upon the Christian religion as not only having been illustrated in the life of Jesus of Nazareth, and a few of the righteous who have gone before us, but I consider it is illustrated in the lives of all those who "fear God and work righteousness." These become sons of God and daughters of God, in the same sense that Jesus was the Son of God. He has been called the Beloved Son. Why was this great distinction conferred upon him? The answer is plain: "Thou hast loved righteousness and hated iniquity: therefore God, even thy God, hath anointed thee with the oil of gladness above thy fellows." He has set us an example of obedience, of faithfulness, and of good works, that we might follow in his steps; and we may overcome the world as he overcame the world, by resisting temptation, and obedience to his Father's will.

I know that many professors of religion look upon it as a great heresy to hold out the idea that Jesus of Nazareth was a man; but I agree with the Scripture testimony concerning him, in which he is spoken of as "man approved of God by signs and wonders which God did by him." I am not denying the *divinity* of Christ, when I say that the *body of Jesus* was no more divine than our bodies are divine. It confessedly had all the attributes of humanity; it was made "in the likeness of men." The same power which sanctified that person and made him pure, will also sanctify us and make us pure. The same "spirit" that descended upon Jesus, will descend upon us; the same word that was there manifested in the flesh, hath also appeared unto us, and all who receive it, according to Scripture testimony, have "power to become the sons of God."

I am not for bringing down this bright example to a level with the irregularities of human conduct. Oh, no! But I am for exalting man above the imperfections and frailties of humanity, to a level with Jesus of Nazareth, for I consider it is the glorious aim of the gospel to bring us up to the same platform of righteousness that we may partake at the same fountain of the Spiritual bread, which cometh down from God out of heaven, and giveth life to the soul. Is not this the doctrine of Jesus? "He that doeth the will of my Father in heaven, the same is my brother, my sister, and my mother."

How beautifully did Jesus call the attention of the people to this power *within themselves,* when he told them, "The kingdom of God cometh not with observation: neither shall they say, Lo, here! or Lo, there! for, behold, the kingdom of God is within you." He spoke of the seed that the sower went forth to sow—of the leaven that was placed in three measures of meal, and by many other parables and figures directed them to the cultivation of the principles of righteousness.

Now, my friends, are we not all satisfied that if the precepts of Jesus were carried out in our daily life; if human conduct was wholly regulated by the principles of love, of mercy, of justice, of truth, that the condition of man would be improved—that there would be far more enjoyment and less misery in the world than there now is in consequence of neglect in cultivating these heaven-born virtues? Is it possible for us to carry out in our lives and conduct these simple elements of the Christian religion? Can we conform to the example and precepts of Jesus? If this be impossible or impracticable, then Christianity is a cunningly devised fable. But we believe it is possible: we believe that the religion of Jesus *may* be carried out in practice: we believe that we can do to others as we would have others do to us: we believe that we can love our enemies, do good to them that hate us, and pray for them that despitefully use us and persecute us. It has been shown unto us what is good, and we know that we are required to fulfil the law of love. Why, then, is not the attention of professing Christians turned more to the *practice* of these things than to the ceremonial part of religion, and a *belief* in their written systems of faith? For what has all this done? It has made sectarians and bigots; it has spread discord, contention and hatred, where all should have been harmony, and peace, and love. See how the peace and harmony of human society has been broken by contending for orthodoxy of opinion. This could never occur if the principles inculcated in the precepts of Jesus were made the standard of righteousness and the rule of life.

I am no sectarian. I cannot believe that God is partial, or that he has neglected any portion of the human family, but that his grace has been extended to all the children of men; in other words, I believe that these principles of righteousness to which I feel concerned to call your attention, have been revealed to all. The Gospel, which Paul declared was preached to every creature, is preached to us, "teaching us that denying ungodliness, and the world's lusts, we should live soberly, righteously, and godly in this present world."

We should not, like the Pharisee of old, surround ourselves with the mantle of self-righteousness, and be ready to say, "I thank God that I am not like other men;" for although we may be permitted to enjoy many privileges that other portions of the human family are not blest with, yet we are accountable for all that we have received. If we have received five talents, we have five more to answer for; and he who had received but one, would have been accepted if that one had been improved. The many favours and blessings we enjoy should fill our hearts with thankfulness to God, and increase our love to our fellow-creatures. With the desire that others may enjoy the blessings of righteousness, there could be no room in our hearts for sectarian bitterness; we would look upon all our fellow-men as children of one common Father, created for the same great purpose, and destined to the same eternity. Oh! when I consider the blessings that would result to mankind if the principles of righteousuess were made the rule of life, I feel concerned for my fellow-creatures, and if I have any mission of the gospel of Christ, it is to call their attention to the cultivation of these, rather than to speculative opinions and written systems of faith. Let godliness be the test of a holy life; let religion be stripped of every thing but practical righteousness. Then charity would take the place of bigotry, and spiritual devotion the place of lifeless forms. Let the sublime precepts of Jesus be obeyed, and the "sword would be beaten into a ploughshare, and the spear into a pruning-hook; nation would no longer lift up sword against nation, neither would men learn war any more." Let us mark the example of him who was accused by the Scribes and Pharisees of being the friend of the publicans and sinners. He went about doing good; he bound up the broken-hearted, proclaimed liberty to the captive, and preached the gospel to the poor. Even the outcasts from society were the objects of his solicitude; he did good to his enemies, and prayed for them even when they were inflicting on him the cruelties of death.

"*Righteousness exalteth a nation.*" But alas! this doctrine is too much overlooked, not only by nations, but by individuals, and it is too little regarded by the popular theology of the present day. Hence with the increase of what is called religion, there is not a corresponding advancement of the peaceable kingdom of Jesus Christ among men. The great profession of religion which is manifesting itself in Sabbath-keeping, in church-going, and a variety of other external observances, would seem to indicate that vital Christianity is spreading in the earth, but when we consider that this *profession of religion* tolerates many irregularities of human conduct, and lends its sanction to some of the greatest evils that ever afflicted the family of man, we are led to fear that it does not embrace the cultivation of the fundamental principles of righteousness.

We hear a great deal said about the conversion of the heathen; we see vast efforts made in circulating the Bible in the earth; we hear of proselytes being multiplied like the drops of the morning. Proselytes to what? To the *practice* of Christianity? No: but to absurd theories and speculative opinions of religion in no way connected with it. The great work of evangelizing the heathen, (as it is called,) seems to be but little more than bringing them to subscribe to certain opinions and doctrines as being fundamental in religion, and when they have endorsed these, they are said to be converted, and are called Christians.

Jesus declared, "By this shall all men know that ye are my disciples, if ye have love one for another." And again: "If any man will be my disciple he must deny self, and take up his cross daily and follow me." Now, it does not appear that there is much concern to spread these great fundamental doctrines of Christianity, from the fact, that while we are going with the *Bible* in one hand, to convert the heathen, we are holding the *sword* in the other.

Many of those who are very earnest in their professions to religion, and zealous in their endeavours to convert the heathen, have such a perverted view of the Christian religion themselves as to believe that it sanctions war, and are by precept and example lending their influence to support this barbarous custom, which had its origin in the depravity of human passions, and is continued from generation to generation, although manifestly at variance with the law of God, written in the hearts of the children of men.

Oh! it is sorrowful when we see the professors of Christianity, and even the professed ministers of Christ, upholding by their testimony and their influence this barbarous practice, either in our own time or in days that are past. How can these be instrumental in spreading the gospel—or in holding up to others a religion that "breathes glory to God in the highest, on earth peace and good will to men?" Would it not be better for them to observe the injunction of Jesus, when he says, "Seest thou the mote in thy brother's eye and beholdest not the beam in thine own eye? Thou hypocrite, first cast the beam out of thine own eye, then shalt thou see more clearly to cast the mote out of thy brother's eye." If we observed this rule, we should see the professors of religion bearing a faithful testimony against the whole custom of war. Then might they with consistency hold out this language to others, "Follow us as we follow Christ." If, instead of loving our enemies, we hate them—instead of blessing, curse them—if, instead of doing good for evil, we hold to the doctrine of repelling evil by evil, our fruits are as unlike the productions of a gospel spirit, as the fruit of the thorn is unlike the grape—or the fruit of the thistle that of the fig tree. I am opposed to war—I wish not to disguise my convictions that it is a gross and palpable violation of the plainest doctrines of Christ. I look upon the custom as being so utterly at variance with the obligations of the gospel, that I shall bear my testimony against it, until this frail tabernacle shall slumber in the stillness of death.

Whatever men may profess, however good or true may be the opinions they have embraced, there is something besides a *belief* in their systems of religion necessary to their salvation. The apostle James, in his day, saw that there was a disposition to depend on faith and belief alone—and to rest satisfied with merely a *name* to religion. "Show me thy faith," says he, "without thy works, and I will show thee my faith by my works. Thou believest there is one God; thou doest well: the devils also believe and tremble. But wilt thou know, O vain man, that faith without works is dead?" So will our faith be dead, unless it produces the fruits of the spirit, which are love, joy, peace, gentleness, meekness, temperance, brotherly kindness and charity.

I have a testimony to bear to the simplicity of the Christian religion. I do not believe that it is so involved in obscurity that we cannot comprehend it. It is plain and simple, and perfectly consistent with the reason of man; for our reason is a gift of the Creator, and divine revelation does not contradict it. I know there are many opinions, promulgated for religious truths, that require a sacrifice of the human understanding—we are asked to believe them, and denounced as infidels if we refuse to subscribe to them, when at the same time these are admitted to be mysteries that the human mind never can understand or comprehend. Take for example the doctrine of the "Trinity." We are told that the Divine Being, who is, "*a spirit*," is composed of three separate and distinct "*persons*." That these three "persons" have equal attributes and equal powers, and that although they are separate and distinct, they are nevertheless one and indivisible!

The doctrine admits of no explanation. It renders the Divine nature wholly incomprehensible, and however much the knowledge of God may be necessary to our present and future well-being, we can never reach it through this dark and gloomy channel.

Has religion any thing to do with such absurdities as this? No: all that we are required to believe and to know, is opened to our understanding by the *light of truth*; that which religion requires is plain and practical, while dogmas so irrational and obscure, are to be ranked with human traditions.

I cannot subscribe to the doctrine, that we are all sinners in consequence of the transgression of our first parents; much less to a scheme of redemption, which has for its object the removal of this supposed innate and original guilt. There is no truth in this idea of a *vicarious atonement*—the innocent suffering for the guilty—and I have no hesitation in calling it a popular superstition. It is not supported by any direct testimony of Jesus Christ, who would not have omitted it had this been the object of his coming, nor would he have told the people of that day, "For this end was I born, and for this cause came I into the world, *that I might bear witness to the truth.*" The idea is inconsistent with reason, and contrary to that great law of cause and effect, which operates with as much certainty in the spiritual as in the physical world. In obedience to this law, if thou doest well, thou shalt be accepted, and if thou doest not well, sin lieth at thy door; and no sacrifice or offering that was ever made *without* thee, can cleanse thee from this sin, and restore thee into the Divine favour. We can only be saved by *resisting temptation*, and by our obedience to the manifestations of the Divine will. We escape the pain of spiritual death—not by any thing that is done without us, but by *ceasing to do evil* and *learning to do well.* The terms of our acceptance with God were expressed long ago in this Scripture declaration, "Let the wicked forsake his ways, and the unrighteous man his thoughts. Let him turn unto the Lord, and he will have mercy on him, and to our God, for he will abundantly pardon,"—and they have never changed.

Now I invite you, my brethren and sisters, to examine these subjects for yourselves. The truth can loose nothing by the most rigid investigation, while error may be detected, and the works of darkness brought to light; and above all things, examine yourselves, whether ye be in the truth, yea or nay. If you feel conscious that you have been forsaking the path of duty, or that you are not faithful stewards over the good gifts bestowed upon you; stop—like prodigal of old—stop, in your wrong career. There is a hand stretched forth for your deliverance, that will lead you back to the path of peace. The divine call is extended to us, "Come unto me all ye that are weary and heavy laden, and I will give you rest." Let us obey that call, we shall thereby promote our present and future well-being; whereas, by persisting in a course of conduct that is evil, the sin, which is a reproach to any people, will rest upon us. Let us "add unto our faith virtue; and to virtue knowledge; and to knowledge temperance; and to temperance patience; and to patience godliness; and to godliness brotherly kindness; and to brotherly kindness charity." "For," says the apostle, "if ye do these things, ye shall never fall." But we shall be introduced into the kingdom of Christ, and when called upon to render an account of our stewardship, be able to adopt the language of the beloved Son, "I have finished the work thou hast given me to do;" and also have the experience of the apostle, that there is laid up for us a "crown of righteousness." Let our religion be an every day religion. Let it consist wholly in the practice of righteousness, and then we will neither be deceived ourselves, nor be able to deceive others. If religion consisted wholly in practical righteousness, no false doctrines could be imposed, no impostor could make any headway among men. There could be no deception, if we adopted the criterion of Jesus—" By their fruits ye shall know them." If we love God, we shall show it by our love one for another. If we are the disciples of Christ, we shall let our light so shine before men, that others seeing our good works, will glorify our Father in heaven.

Oh! for more such Christianity as this, in which the precepts of the gospel are fulfilled. Then would cease the conflict of opinions and the strife of tongues, that has arrayed brother against brother, and sect against sect, and Divine love would exert its holiest influence among the children of men. Let it begin with us. Let our hearts become filled with these divine principles—and let them be expanded in love to our fellow creatures and our God.

Thus shall we be instrumental in hastening the day when the " Mountain of the Lord's house shall be established on the top of the mountains, and all nations shall flow unto it," and this universal voice be heard, " Come brother, come sister, let us go up together to the mountain of the Lord, to the house of the God of Jacob; for He will teach us of his ways, and we will walk in his paths."

SERMON III.

DELIVERED AT FRIENDS' MEETING AT CHERRY STREET, PHILADELPHIA, ELEVENTH MONTH 6TH, 1849.

I HAVE remembered, since we have been together, I believe with deeper instruction than I have ever before known, the account furnished in the Scriptures of a meeting of the disciples on a certain occasion, when it is said, that Jesus came and stood in the midst and saith unto them, "Peace be unto you." I was led to query whether that account referred to one meeting of this character only, and whether it were possible for us to witness, as these disciples did, the presence of Jesus Christ. It seems to me, the same power which overshadowed that meeting, and made it a season of consolation to these disciples, that converted them and blessed them, continues still to be revealed to man, in agreement with the promise "where two or three are met together in my name, there will I be in the midst of them." Without this sensible evidence of the Divine presence in our midst, our assembling in this manner will be profitless and comfortless—it will be but an empty form that cannot satisfy those desires of the immortal spirit, which are constantly prompting the soul onward in its progress towards heaven. It was on the occasion to which I have referred, that these disciples received the commission "Go ye, therefore, and teach all nations, baptising them in the name of the Father, and of the

Son, and of the Holy Ghost; teaching them to observe all things, whatsoever I have commanded you: and lo, I am with you alway, even unto the end of the world." The commission and promise here given, can scarcely be understood or appreciated amidst the traditional views and opinions which have so generally obtained, concerning the coming of Christ. If we look beyond the figurative mode of expression to the reality, which I have no doubt the writer of this history meant to convey, if we mistake not the shadow for the substance, nor substitute the type for its antitype, the account of the circumstances immediately preceding and attending this meeting of the disciples, may become very instructive to us. Jesus, while he was engaged among them in the work of his mission, told them, "It is expedient for you that I go away; for if I go not away, the comforter will not come unto you." He saw the necessity of turning their minds from an outward person to a Divine Power, from that which consisted in flesh and blood, to that which was spirit, for according to his own testimony, "the flesh profiteth nothing, it is the spirit that quickeneth." Hence, also he said unto them, "I will pray the Father, and he shall give you another comforter, that he may abide with you forever; even the spirit of truth, whom the world cannot receive, because it seeth him not, neither knoweth him: but ye know him; for he dwelleth with you and shall be in you. I will not leave you comfortless; I will come to you." When he gave this promise, he certainly had no allusion to his outward person, he could not have meant that this was the comforter that would appear and abide with them forever. Far otherwise; the figurative style which so much abounds in these writings is calculated to mislead, unless we are careful to give the words and expressions that are used an appropriate spiritual meaning.

It is clear that the disciples, like the great mass of the professors of Christianity in the present day, were so outward in their views and expectations, that they did not perceive the meaning of Jesus, for one of them put the query to him in this wise, "Lord how is it that thou wilt manifest thyself unto us, and not unto the world?" Seeing that they did not understand the spiritual import of his words, Jesus endeavoured to lead them to a more spiritual view of the manifestation of Christ in the flesh; in which they could comprehend it as the "wisdom of God, and the power of God," the word by which the worlds were made. Thus he led them to look for Christ within them, and in reply to the inquiry of Judas, he answered, "If any man love me he will keep my words; and my Father will love him, and we will come and make our abode with him." Here he directed them to a spiritual manifestation, in which he should appear as the quickening spirit, and word of life to the soul. For this same word that dwelt in the flesh in the person of Jesus of Nazareth, as certainly is manifested in us, and to every rational creature under heaven for the same blessed purpose that it dwelt in him, to raise us to an equality with the angels of God.

To this word of life, the gospel invites us in the affectionate language, "Come unto me all ye that are weary and heavy laden, and I will give you rest."

What are the views of the great mass of Christian professors concerning Christ? Are they not very outward and traditional? Is not the attention of the people directed back to Jesus of Nazareth, rather than to his inward and spiritual appearing—from the operation of the spirit, to a dependence upon the outward person? While such views of Christ are entertained, as are incompatible with the spiritual nature of the gospel, how can we hope for the increase of that kingdom, which brings "Glory to God in the highest, peace on earth, and good will to men?" This can never be realized, until Christ is witnessed as a ruling power and principle in man, governing all his actions by its benign influence, opening the path of duty before him, and showing him what he shall do, and what he shall leave undone. When, therefore, the disciples had their understandings opened on the occasion to which I have alluded, by the manifestation of Christ, they received the command, "Go ye forth teaching all nations," accompanied with the promise, "Lo, I am with you alway unto the end of the world." What now was it that was to be with them always? The power that opened their understandings and comforted them with the language, "Peace be unto you." Then, and not till then, they realized the truth of the promise, "I will pray the Father, and he will send you another comforter." But see how it was when Jesus was taken from them: mark what occurred when those faithful women went to the place where he lay, whom their souls had loved, with the anxious inquiry, "Who shall roll us away the stone from the door of the sepulchre?" "Behold there was a great earthquake; for the angel of the Lord descended from heaven, and came and rolled back the stone from the door and sat upon it, his countenance was as lightning, and his raiment white as snow." Then was the doctrine of Christs' spiritual appearing opened unto them, and they were prepared to go to the disciples with the joyful tidings, "He is risen from the dead."

Are not the professors of Christianity now, like those faithful women, seeking the living among the dead? No doubt in the sincerity and fullness of their hearts, many are looking to the outward person that was crucified and laid in the sepulchre, and it will require the same earthquake to shake their dependence upon an outward Redeemer; the same angel of the Lord must desend from heaven, and roll back this stone of tradition from the door, and sit upon it, that it may no longer prevent them from beholding Christ in his inward and spiritual appearing, as the eternal word and ever present Saviour.

This society has been distinguished from other religious sects, by holding up these views of the spiritual coming of Christ. Have we known him to be in our midst as the crowning power of our assemblies—has this power subdued and sanctified our hearts—has it united us together in the fellowship of the gospel, and commissioned us to go forth "teaching all nations," that others may be baptised into this power, which shall abide with them always? Oh, if this were the case, what meetings we should witness; our religious assemblies would be blessed with the Divine presence, and we should be clothed with authority to be witnesses of Christ in "Jerusalem, in Judea, and the uttermost parts of the earth." It is not enough, that we observe the form of meeting together, we must witness Divine Goodness to overshadow us, we must know our hearts made pure, and must feel the peaceable spirit of Jesus, we must bear one another's burdens, and so fulfill the law of Christ.

A state like this is always profitable, but when it fails to be attained, the great end of religious association can never be answered. We must so witness the spirit of Jesus Christ, and be baptised unto the power of the gospel, that we can enter into sympathy one with another; then if a brother be overtaken with a fault, (and we are all thus liable,) those who are spiritually minded, would seek to restore such a one in the spirit of love and of good will, remembering themselves lest they also be tempted.

Oh! my friends, have we reflected on the duties which the gospel imposes upon us? By our profession we are holding up to the world these cardinal doctrines of Christ, and we should so live up to them, that others seeing our *good works* would be led to glorify our Father which is in heaven. There is something in the view that Christ is with us *always*, that is full of instruction and encouragement. He is continually leading us to faithfulness in little things. He qualifies us to fulfil the duties connected with every day and every hour—these duties will be presented to us, when we lie down, when we rise up, and when we walk by the way.

We may sometimes overlook the requirements of truth and duty while we are waiting for what we may be pleased to call some greater demonstration, that we are invited to this work—the silent operation and promptings of the principle within ourselves, which is man's only true enlightener, may be neglected, and we throw off the responsibility which attaches to faithfulness in little things, while we are waiting for some great light to accomplish some supposed great end.

The religion of Jesus, my friends, is to be advanced by our faithfulness in little things, in the performance of every-day duties; some of these lead us to examine the state of our own minds, others to fulfil the obligations we are under to our Father in heaven, and to our fellow-creatures upon earth. This is what makes the Christian; to fill up faithfully all the relations of life; to make our religion of that practical character, that in all our conduct amongst men we shall exhibit the spirit of the gospel, and imitate the beloved of God in justice, mercy, truth, humility, brotherly kindness and charity.

Oh! here is the commission that Christ ever gives —this is the call we have received—the work whereunto we are sent—and the prayer of my spirit is, that we may none of us be found standing idle in the market places, with the paltry plea, "No man hath hired us." Such excuses do not correspond with the promises of the gospel, but are at variance with the great doctrine that was taught to the disciples; "Lo, I am with you alway, even unto the end of the world."

"If any man have not the spirit of Christ he is none of his;" but this spirit is not withheld from any of us. Let us seek to be more and more imbued with it, till our minds are clothed with love to God and love to each other.

We may ask ourselves the question, whether love abounds as it ought to do, among a people professing the religion of Christ? Whether we have faithfully discharged the duties it enjoins, and whether we have laboured one with another in the peaceable spirit and wisdom of Jesus, for each other's good?

The answer will be found within ourselves. Such inquiries will stimulate us to action, and may, as we are faithful to our convictions of duty, often lead us, as Ananias was led of old, when he was sent on this high mission to one who was praying in Tarsus, with this encouraging language; "Brother Saul, receive thy sight." But I fear the spirit of the gospel is wanted more among us than it exists. Let us search our own hearts. I am willing to be one with you in the labour, that every root of bitterness may be destroyed, and the devil of hatred be overcome by the angel of love.

Let every thing that worketh an abomination or maketh a lie be removed, and then, as it was said, Jesus appeared first unto her, out of whom he had cast seven devils, so, when we meet together in the name of Christ, we shall hear his voice in the midst of us, speaking the language, "Peace be unto you."

SERMON IV.

DELIVERED AT FRIENDS' MEETING, WOODBURY, N. J., ELEVENTH MONTH 15TH, 1849,

One of the strongest proofs to my mind of the Divine authority of the gospel of Christ, is disclosed by the fact, that it is constantly urging upon us to leave the things that are behind, and press forward towards a higher state of experience and enjoyment of the things that pertain to the kingdom of heaven: and, also, from the fact, that it assigns no limit to the progression of the Immortal Spirit short of its complete union with the Divine fountain from which it sprang.

It holds out to us that we are progressive beings, that we may advance step by step in the knowledge of God, and of the unspeakable riches and treasures of his kingdom, of the increase of which there shall never be an end.

What we see continually illustrated in the natural, is shown by the gospel to be the beautiful order of the spiritual world; and this progression that is promoted by it, proves it to be of Divine origin. It addresses itself to us as it did to one formerly, who, when describing his state of mind, says, "I was in the spirit on the Lord's day," and there came an angel unto him, saying, "Come hither, I will show thee the bride, the Lamb's wife. And he carried me away in the spirit to a great and high mountain, and showed me that great city, the Holy Jerusalem, descending from God out of heaven."

It is the same gospel that was preached to man in the beginning, and is still preached to every rational creature under heaven. For, as in the outward firmament, God hath appointed no new light to illuminate the outward world, so in the spiritual kingdom, Christ hath been the enlightener of man, from the very period of time when his Creator breathed into him that "breath of life" which made him "a living soul." This Word, manifested in the flesh, is not to be limited or confined to its appearance in the person of Jesus of Nazareth, for there is abundant Scripture testimony going to show, that the same Power and Word that was manifested in Him also spoke to our first parents, instructed Patriarchs, Prophets and Apostles, and is revealed to us for the same blessed purpose, to raise us above the earthly into the heavenly nature, to an equality with the angels of God.

"Come hither, I will show thee the bride, the Lamb's wife." These are figurative expressions, abounding throughout the Scriptures, but they point to a reality, to a power and principle within that will teach us as man never taught; and to a state of heavenly-mindedness that may be attained by our obedience to Christ.

This gospel also addresses itself to our rational understanding; its convictions are rendered so intelligible, that all may comprehend it with sufficient clearness to perceive their duty, and to know that their work consists in walking in the light that is thus made manifest, that they may become children of the light and of the day. Now, my friends, have we considered that we are favoured with the light of Christ, precisely as the righteous in past ages have been before us!

The same angel that John saw, is also addressing itself to us, and inviting us to come up in our heavenly journey; that we also may be shown that great city, the holy Jerusalem, "descending out of heaven from God," which consists in a state of righteousness and purity.

Have we considered that we are placed in a position so favourable to our advancement to a state of perfection? It is well for us to examine our high privileges, and properly appreciate them. For if we lightly value them, we shall not be likely to improve the opportunities we have, or rightly occupy the gifts which have been bestowed upon us. Thus we may pass on through life, and finally reach the end of our stewardship, without being able to render any better account of our progress, than the unprofitable servant who put his master's talent in a napkin, and buried it in the earth.

I am not about to hold up religion as a terror. I have no idea of serving God through fear of judgments to come. This is not the character of the gospel! Its language is, "Come unto me all ye that are weary and heavy laden, and I will give you rest. Take my yoke upon you and learn of me, for my yoke is easy, and my burden is light." I would hold it up as something that is so lovely in itself, as to make it attractive and inviting, as something that enables us to overcome every sin that doth so easily beset us, and elevate our condition step by step in the scale of improvement, till we become united with the inhabitants of that city, "which needs not the light of the sun, nor of the moon to shine in it, for the glory of God doth enlighten it, and the Lamb is the light thereof."

What then is the Christian progress, and how shall it be made to put us in possession of the treasures of a heavenly kingdom? We must give all diligence to make our calling and election sure, by adding to our "faith virtue, to virtue knowledge, to knowledge patience, to patience temperance, to temperance godliness, to godliness brotherly kindness, and to brotherly kindness charity."

It is by continuing to do these things, that the apostle says we shall never fall, but shall be made fruitful in the knowledge of Jesus Christ. This is the only saving knowledge of Christ. It is known by these fruits. This is the religion that I would hold up to our view, because it is constantly inviting us to go on unto perfection. It is not a religion of opinion, or outward ceremony, it is not confined to any particular form of devotion, it cannot be reached by subscribing to any particular written creed. The only religion that is profitable to man, is that which is embraced with sincerity from a conviction of the understanding, and put in practice in the every day relations of life. We may have our beautiful theories of faith, and persuade ourselves as some did formerly, that this will save us; but, says the apostle James, "What doth it profit, my brethren, though a man say he hath faith, and have not works? Can faith save him? Faith without works is dead." We may be very zealous in defending the orthodoxy of our opinions, and in building up our systems of religion on the traditions of men, but if we are not carrying out in the practice of life the vital principles of righteousness, all our theorizing and creed-making will only be like the righteousness of the Scribes and Pharisees, of whom Jesus spoke, when he said to the people of his time, "Except your righteousness exceed the righteousness of the Scribes and Pharisees, ye shall in no wise enter into the kingdom of heaven."

Religion, to be useful, must be practical. Our Father in Heaven, regarding with indifference what men so often consider essential to a holy life, an adherence to certain opinions, and the observance of outward ceremonies, looks at the heart, and condescends to dwell in the mind that is humble and contrited before him. The soul that feels there is none in heaven but him, or in all the earth that is like unto him, witnesses the truth of the declaration, "Behold the tabernacle of God is with man, and God shall dwell in them, and he will be their God, and they shall serve him."

Now if religion embraces the practical fulfilment of all the duties of life, we shall see that it increases the amount of human happiness, binds man to his fellow, and extends the great law of love "from sea to sea, and from the rivers to the ends of the earth." Its influence over human conduct should soften the heart, regulate the affections, subdue the "lusts of the flesh, the lusts of the eye, and the pride of life," and give us a victory over the world. Oh! it will enable us to overcome the sins that doth most easily beset us, and there is no victory greater than this. To overcome one of the enemies of our household, which are the sins and follies that beset our path, is a victory of infinitely more value than the mightiest triumph that ever was achieved amidst the "confused noise of the warrior and garments rolled in blood." "He that is slow to anger is greater than the mighty, and he that ruleth his own spirit, than he that taketh a city."

How many such victories might we obtain by watchfulness, obedience, and prayer, by regulating our thoughts, and bringing every desire and temperament of mind into the harmony of the Divine will. This is the Christian's work, and in the accomplishment of it, we progress onward in our heavenly journey, till we reach this holy Jerusalem, the city of our God.

Oh! my young friends, this is a subject that interests you in a very especial manner. I would affectionately ask you to give it due consideration. Religion is not to be your dread, but your delight; it is not to deprive you of any permanent good, or lessen any enjoyment that God in his infinite wisdom designed you to realize. He who has made the world on which we dwell, subservient to one prevailing principle of beauty and order, has invited us to behold in his workmanship examples worthy of imitation. We discover in every thing around us, traces of the order, benevolence, and omnipotence of God. "The invisible things of him from the creation of the world are clearly seen, being understood by the things that are made." Shall we see these examples of order, benevolence and goodness, these traces of an Infinite Mind written in the outward creation, and overlook that still more glorious revelation of himself, in which he has appeared in our hearts, for the blessed purpose of elevating us to a condition to enjoy his glory? I would encourage you, my brethren and sisters, to appreciate and cultivate this noble endowment of the Creator. It is of more value than any thing this world can give you, and is capable of vast improvement. It is my conviction, that infinite progression is an attribute of immortality, and while I entertain this belief, I must regard these revelations of God in the present life, as the commencement of a higher order of being, which shall continue to enlarge and expand, when we shall lay aside these frail tenements of dust. With this hope before us, death is disarmed of its sting, and the grave of its victory.

I invite you, therefore, my young friends, calmly and seriously to examine the subject for yourselves. Look upon religion as something that is inviting you above the lower enjoyments of this world, and cultivate the talents that God has given you. You are reminded that the harvest is plenteous, and invited to labour, that you may reap a rich reward. The angels of God bring to you glad tidings of great joy, and fill your spirits with a desire to know more of his infinite attributes and perfections. Live up to your convictions of duty; lay the foundation of your spiritual building upon these revelations of truth to your own souls, and the superstructure that will be raised upon it, will be like the city which John saw, "having on the north three gates, on the east three gates, on the south three gates, and on the west three gates"—a beautiful figure, showing that the avenues through which truth, and light, and knowledge shall enter, are abundant on every side.

Let Christ within be your hope of glory. Follow not after the traditions and opinions of men, which are often embraced without examination, without regard to their applicability, as a rule of human conduct, and often at variance with reason, one of the noblest gifts of God. Regard the Divine voice to your own minds as the highest oracle of truth, and if you would go on unto perfection, above all things fail not to give heed to this "angel of light," that is inviting you onward and upward in your heavenly journey, in the beautiful language "Come up hither, and I will show thee the bride, the Lamb's wife."

SERMON V.

DELIVERED AT FRIENDS' MEETING, DARBY, ELEVENTH MONTH 25TH, 1849.

"What will it profit a man, if he shall gain the whole world, and lose his own soul?" These words of Jesus have been presented to the view of my mind as being full of instruction, and worthy of our individual consideration. When we consider that every accountable and immortal being that is brought into existence, is the immediate offspring of its Divine author, we shall not wonder that Jesus should have placed the value of the soul higher than even the possession of the whole world. *To be*, and to know that we are in possession of an immortal spirit, is to have an evidence of that link in the great chain that connects the present with the future, and unites man to his Maker. We have received our spiritual nature immediately from God. It constitutes the germ of immortality and eternal life, which under the blessed influence of the gospel of Christ, is capable of unlimited growth and enlargement. Taking this view, we shall see the force of the expression of Jesus, "What will it profit a man, if he shall gain the whole world, and lose his own soul?" It is a question of vital importance to our present and future well-being, to know that we are in *possession* of a nature that does not die, when the tabernacle in which it is contained shall return to the dust from which it was taken; and it is equally important that we should improve a gift, bearing upon it the proof of divine origin. If we read attentively and understandingly the beautiful parables of Jesus, we shall find that many of them have a direct reference to this subject; that through these he endeavoured to instruct his disciples in the nature of the growth of the immortal spirit, from the state of a germ in which it was bestowed, to that state in which it becomes perfected in the knowledge of its Author.

When Jesus compared the kingdom of heaven to "a grain of mustard seed," or to the "seed that a sower went forth to sow," or a "little leaven hid in three measures of meal," he represents it as something small in its first appearance, but which is capable of being cultivated and improved, by the continual addition of the experience of the things belonging to that kingdom. The grain of mustard seed, unless it were placed in a position favourable to its growth, would be of no further value than a single grain, but we see it contains within itself the elements of its own reproduction. When the soil upon which it falls is prepared to receive and nourish it, it is then that it brings forth the stem, the branches, the blossom, and finally the fruit fully ripe, and this process is continually repeated. Thus the outward world furnishes an illustration of the growth to be experienced by our spiritual nature, until that germ of the Divine life, which is immediately bestowed by the Author of our being, and which constitutes us beings, "made in the image of God," has expanded and brought forth those fruits of "righteousness, peace and joy in the Holy Spirit," in which the apostle declares the kingdom of heaven consists.

We shall lose our own souls, so far as the enjoyment of those things is to be realized, if we neglect this kind of culture, for our spiritual nature can only expand and yield these fruits as it is cultivated and improved.

These parables of Jesus are akin to the figure of the Garden of Eden, in which man is placed, with authority to dress and keep the trees of the garden, and partake of the fruit of all except the "tree of the knowledge of evil." Thus we have parables and figures throughout the Scriptures, all pointing us to the improvement of a treasure that we have in "earthen vessels," and as this is improved, we advance from one mansion of the Heavenly Father's house to another, for according to the testimony of Jesus, it is declared, "In my Father's house are *many* mansions, if it were not so, I would have told you, I go to prepare a place for you, that where I am there ye may be also."

The professed belief among Christians is, that the soul cannot be saved without Christ, and if this doctrine were carried out in practice, we should see wonderful illustrations of this growth to which I have alluded, in the knowledge of the Lord spreading from sea to sea, and from the rivers to the ends of the earth. If men really believed that their salvation depended on their likeness to Christ, all the wrongs and evils of unrighteousness would cease, and the kingdom of God would come on earth as it is in heaven.

But unhappily men do not in reality believe that they are to be saved by their likeness to Christ, so much as by their opinions concerning him. Hence the great doctrine of salvation by Christ, and the souls advancement from stature to stature, till it attains to the state of a "man in Christ Jesus" is not fully understood; and in consequence, the fruits of the spirit, which are love, peace, joy, charity, and all the heavenly virtues, do not correspond with the great profession of religion that is made among men.

We know these fruits will appear wherever men witness salvation by Christ; but while they are depending on their opinions concerning a Saviour, they will never be brought out of darkness into the light of the gospel day; neither will the church ever be brought out of the wilderness of lifeless forms and ceremonies, to behold the beauty of that temple where

God is worshipped in spirit. Upon this subject, men are losing their own souls, or at least giving them up to the keeping of others. Look over the religious world, and see how many thousands and tens of thousands of our fellow beings are taught to look for their spiritual bread, their knowledge of God, of Christ, of the kingdom of heaven, to the teachings of men. Resting satisfied with a name to live, and persuading themselves that their opinions concerning religion, Christ and God are true, and therefore they have accomplished all they have to do, in the work of the souls advancement, and relying upon the testimony of others for authority, are willing to leave unread the great volume of truth which Christ opens to his followers. Happily would it be for the professors of Christianity, if they would seek for higher evidence of the presence of Christ, than the declarations of men, and they would find the promise, "Lo, I am with you always," verified in their own experience. There is an incident related in the Scriptures of one of the disciples of Jesus, that I have viewed with instruction and encouragement. It is the account of Thomas, who is commonly considered an unbeliever, because he was not willing to rest his hope of salvation upon what other men said or saw. He was not willing to be satisfied with the testimony of his brethren, when they said unto him, "We have seen the Lord," but wanted a higher demonstration of the Divine presence, than could be drawn from any human authority. This is apparent from the language he used, which, though highly figurative and metaphorical, clearly conveys the honest intention and earnest desire of his mind, to receive an evidence equal to that which the disciples themselves had; "Except I shall see in his hands the print of the nails, and put my finger into the print of the nails, and thrust my hand into his side, I will not believe." Mark now, the wonderful condescension and goodness of God towards this honest inquirer; all the evidence he asked for was granted him; for Christ appears, and addresses himself to his state in language that he could understand; "Reach hither thy finger and behold my hands, and reach hither thy hand and thrust it into my side, and be not faithless, but believing."

Thus was he enlightened by the same power that opened the understanding of his brethren on another occasion, to comprehend and behold the Divine presence, and while enjoying this clear and heavenly illumination, he could worship in the language, "My Lord and my God."

Now if there were more unbelievers of this description, I doubt not there would be more devout worshippers in the Christian church, for I believe the same undeniable evidence, as clear and precisely of the same character, would be furnished to us, as was furnished to Thomas and the rest of these disciples, if rightly sought after. I am aware that many overlook the encouragement and instruction which the record of this event is designed to afford, by supposing that it was the outward body of Jesus, that Thomas and the other disciples saw. I do not so understand it, and it is only leading us from the inward and saving, to outward and carnal views of

Christ to hold such doctrine. It was a spiritual manifestation to the disciples, precisely as he is manifested to us. While we are in possession of an immortal soul, he dwells near us, and the language that was uttered formerly remains to be as true now as it was then; "Behold I stand at the door and knock, if any man will hear my voice and open unto me, I will come in and sup with him, and he shall sup with me." If we rest satisfied with other men's opinions, we cease to be thinking beings, we cease to ask, that we may receive; to knock, that it may be opened unto us; and failing to inquire for ourselves, our understandings are not opened to comprehend the sublime realities of the kingdom of heaven. We should not separate the word *Christ* from the word *power;* they are and ever have been the same thing. He is spoken of as the "light that lighteth every man that cometh into the world," opening the path of duty before him, warning him against evil, and justifying him for doing good. He is the power that enables man to resist temptation, to overcome evil, to go on his way from glory to glory. We should confine our views of him entirely to the operation of this power within ourselves, that we may have such an evidence of his presence, as will enable us to say from living experience, "I know that my Redeemer lives, and because he lives, we shall live also."

In the parable of the sower, Jesus illustrated the goodness of the great Husbandman, in the universal distribution of the good seed, the seed of a spiritual nature; and it is for us to say, whether that seed shall fall upon stony ground, by the way-side, among thorns, or upon soil prepared for its reception and growth. Let all the energies of our minds, instead of being coverted into swords and spears, be converted into ploughshares and pruning-hooks, to cultivate the ground for the reception and growth of this seed, in a new heaven and a new earth wherein dwelleth righteousness. Then we shall see that the value of the soul increases as it expands in the knowledge of its Author.

Our views of the Divine mind should not be such as to shut him out from the present life, leading us only to anticipate a knowledge of Him when we shall have passed beyond the limits of time. Oh, no; he is not far from every one of us, seeing that "in Him we live and move, and have our being."

That same benevolent Being who has spread out before us the visible world as a monument of his wisdom, power and goodness, has also furnished to his rational, intelligent creation, a witness of himself. We are, therefore, called to a knowledge of God and Christ now; such a knowledge that will regulate our thoughts and conduct, purify the heart, sanctify the affections, and elevate the soul into the enjoyment of the Divine harmony here, and lay the foundation of a well-grounded hope of its continuance in the world to come.

But, my friends, this can only be realized as we continue to possess and occupy our own souls, by improving the gifts and talents committed to our care.

Now, if there is nothing of sufficient value to be received in exchange for our spiritual nature, and if this constitutes the connecting link that unites us to the Infinite Mind, does it not follow, even though we look no further than the present life, that if we lose our own souls we cannot realize the enjoyment arising from union with God.

We should embrace the religion of Jesus, because it puts us in possession of the joys of heaven in the present as well as the future world. But I have no idea of people being driven to embrace religion, or any system of belief or opinion (as is often the case) through fear of judgments to come, for this only tends to drive men into darkness and error.

Religion should be held up, and especially to the young mind, as something that is cheerful and joyous in its character; something that shall make it happier every day and every hour; something that shall preserve it from all evil and secure to it all that is good. I have no faith in that dark and gloomy theology which terrifies the mind of the child, by insisting upon its total depravity, and the absence of a pure and undefiled spirit; that holds up to it a fear of death and of imaginary torments beyond the grave, to frighten it into religion. Religion should be held up to the view of the child in the language of Jesus: "Suffer little children to come unto me and forbid them not, for of such is the kingdom of heaven." It should be represented as a path shining brighter and brighter unto the perfect day; such a view will correspond with the soul's advancement from one mansion of the heavenly Father's house to another; and our minds should ever be impressed with the conviction, that the moment we turn aside from this path, we are on the downward course—a course strewed with briars and thorns, and which, as it is pursued, leads through all the wanderings of folly, misery, and wretchedness, and finally to ruin. In presenting these views of religion, I shall not be understood, that it ever leads to the indulgence of any hurtful thing. It will control every passion, and set bounds to the indulgence of every propensity belonging to the animal nature of man, and a moment's reflection will satisfy us of the hurtful tendency of improper indulgence in these. The view I wish to convey is, that religion, in regulating our lives, and bringing the animal propensities under the control and dominion of the spiritual man, will deprive us of no real good; but that it will render life a scene of enjoyment; it opens to us the creation of God, as springing from its author, and invites us to look upon his works as the monuments of his infinite wisdom and power: it invites us to look within ourselves for the traces of his omnipotence and omnipresence; that in the spirit's sanctuary we may hold communion with a Being whom the heaven of heavens cannot contain, but who condescends to dwell with the pure in heart, the humble and contrite spirit. Oh! my friends, could we keep such views of religion before us, and contemplate the nature and value of the immortal soul, we should be encouraged to press forward till we experience those joys and blessed realities which the righteous of all past time have witnessed, by walking by the same rule, and minding the same thing. Like the beloved Son, we shall also, as we are led by the spirit of God, become "heirs of God, and joint heirs with Christ." We should then experience a likeness to Christ, in the state of meekness, humility, love, universal charity for all mankind, and an enlarged philanthropy to which we shall have attained. Love to God, and to our fellow-creatures would be the secret spring of all our actions, and all our works would correspond.

When mankind come to embrace these views, there will be fruits of righteousness, peace on earth, and good-will to men, such as the world never yet has witnessed, for this doctrine has for its object the growth of man's spiritual nature, from the germ-like state in which it was bestowed, until it prepares him to enjoy the society of saints and angels in the kingdom of heaven.

SERMON VI.

DELIVERED AT BRISTOL MEETING, ON FIRST-DAY, TWELFTH MONTH 16TH, 1849.

If I have a clear understanding of what the Christian religion is, I discover nothing in it but what is plain and easily understood; nothing that is inconsistent with right reason; nothing that involves an absurdity or contradiction; but, on the other hand, it is a religion that is adapted to the wants of man under all circumstances in which he may be placed, to whatever nation, kindred, tongue, or people he may belong.

It is a religion that is based upon the universal benevolence of our Father in heaven, who is no respector of persons, but who reveals his law to *all* the children of men, and all who live in obedience to it, as manifested to them, are accepted of him.

Such was the religion that the blessed Jesus promulgated amongst men, and we cannot be conversant with his declarations, his precepts and his parables, without perceiving that the great object of his mission was not to fill the ears of the people with abstract notions and speculative opinions, nor to institute external forms and ceremonies, but to direct them within themselves, to what he properly calls the Kingdom of Heaven, that they might be instructed in the way of their duty; and by obedience to these instructions, thus inwardly received, they should walk as he walked, in a state of acceptance with their heavenly Father, and thus overcome the world, and be prepared to sit down with him upon his throne, even as he overcame and sat down with his Father upon his throne. In the instructive exhortation which he gave them, "What I say unto one I say unto all, watch and pray, and that continually, lest ye enter into temptation," he pointed out the origin of evil, and incited them to cultivate that good seed of the kingdom of heaven, which would bring forth fruit in due season, and declared, that by these fruits they should be known as his disciples.

It seems to me, the great object of preaching and of religion, is to direct us individually within ourselves; that we also may understand the great truth to which Jesus alludes, when he spoke of the kingdom of heaven, as the good seed which a heavenly husbandman had sown in his spiritual kingdom, and of which an apostle also testified, when he declared, "Ye are the temples of the living God, and the spirit of God dwelleth in you." When we come to know ourselves, we shall discover that all the evil which afflicts the family of man, owes its origin to his disobedience and transgression of the Divine laws; and the first step towards our salvation from sin, is rightly to understand where evil has its origin. The apostle, no doubt, saw the necessity of this in his time, and hence he makes use of this language; "Let no man say when he is tempted, I am tempted of God, for God cannot be tempted with evil, neither tempteth he any man: but every man is tempted when he is drawn away of his own lust and enticed: then when lust hath conceived, it bringeth forth sin; and sin, when it is finished, bringeth forth death." In the view here given by the apostle, the divine character is not only cleared from any participation in the evil that is in the world, but its origin is traced to man's yielding to temptation, or to his disobedience to that law that would have kept him from falling, and preserved him faultless in the sight of his Maker. Hence we see the fitness of the command of Jesus, to watch and pray, and that continually, lest ye enter into temptation. This, my friends, is a great duty, the first step towards our preservation from evil; and Jesus knowing that the soul of man (that nature which alone can rise or fall, as it regards spiritual things,) was pure as it came from its Divine author, therefore warned them to watch lest they entered into temptation. The gospel teaches us that we are not only to guard the avenues of the heart against the admission of evil, but to labour in the attainment of good, as Jesus illustrated in this beautiful parable of the sower sowing good seed, wherein he pointed out, not innate depravity, but original virtue, and angelic purity. It seems to me, that if the preaching of the present age had this end in view, that there would soon be a manifest advancement in the religious world, towards a more exalted state of righteousness than now exists. I know that many will shrink back and hide themselves behind the curtain of a dark and mysterious theology, at the very thought of there being any thing in man that is of a divine character, that is pure and undefiled, for the opposite doctrine is taught, that we are by nature the children of wrath; that we are aliens to God, to truth, to holiness, and to every thing that is pure. A doctrine the very opposite of that which the apostle taught, who declared, that sin originated in every man as he *was drawn away of his own lust and enticed,* and not in consequence of the sins or transgressions of another, as imposed upon mankind by the popular creeds; and the religious world is filled with theological fictions concerning the origin of evil, in which man is represented to be a sinner by nature, coming into the world in a state of separation from God; and sin is attributed, not so much to our own transgressions as to some supposed guilt entailed upon us by the transgressions of others. And what does all this appear to be for? Why so much exertion to prove the *total depravity* of man?

It is for no other purpose than to magnify the necessity of a scheme of redemption as full of absurdity as it is possible for error to make it—the doctrine of the vicarious atonement. Instead of religion being held up as something that is plain and easily understood, it is made to consist of erroneous opinions concerning the origin of evil, and of man's redemption from it by the outward sacrifice of Jesus Christ. I would not be considered as casting uncharitable reflections upon any of my fellow professors, who may entertain opinions like these; all I ask is that I may not be required to subscribe to doctrines which, in my view, are utterly repugnant to every principle of justice, mercy, truth and love. Far be it from me to condemn my brother or my sister who may entertain different views on these subjects. While I honestly dissent from opinions that I cannot adopt, without a sacrifice of reason and a disregard of the convictions of truth on my own mind, I wish not to condemn any, but I must bear my testimony to what I consider the erroneous opinions that are promulgated as a part of the religion of Jesus. My object is mainly to enforce the observance of those principles of righteousness and of truth, without which no man, whatever his name to religion may be, can ever stand accepted in the Divine sight. Religion, in my view, does not consist in our systems of faith, in subscribing to any particular creed, or in the observance of any external rituals. It requires something more than all this. "Pure religion, undefiled before God is this, to visit the fatherless and the widow in their afflictions, and keep ourselves unspotted from the world." This was the religion of our great example, and it should become ours. He was no respecter of persons. His mission of gospel love was not to a few, but to all. He embraced within his holy mission the very ends of the earth. "Come unto me all ye that are weary and heavy laden and I will give you rest; and take my yoke upon you, and learn of me, and ye shall find rest to your souls." What is comprehended in the command, "Take my yoke upon you?" Is it not our daily obedience to that "law of the spirit of life in Christ Jesus," which Paul declared "made him free from the law of sin and death?"

If we are to be preserved from falling into temptation and a snare, we must watch unto prayer; if we are to be set free from sin and death, it must be by our obedience to this "law of the spirit of life in Christ Jesus." Now there is no mystery in this doctrine, for there is as certainly a manifestation of the Divine will to mankind now as there ever was since the first period of human existence. And this will is manifested to us in the same manner that it has ever been revealed to man, *through a spiritual medium.* The same voice who addressed to Adam the language, "Where art thou," discovered to him the state and condition of his soul; pointed out the cause and consequences of his alienation from God, and that the only hope of his return consisted in obedience to the quickening operation of the Spirit, which is represented under the figure of a "flaming sword turning every way to guard the way of the tree of life." This voice speaks to us in precisely the same manner. We are not to be so outward as to suppose that the Almighty Jehovah was ever seen with mortal eye, or his voice heard with mortal ear. Jesus declared, "No man hath seen God at any time, the only begotten of the Father he hath revealed him." When we read of the voice of the Lord being heard in the cool of the day, or accompanied by the thunderings and lightnings of Sinai—speaking to patriarchs, prophets and apostles; when we read of Moses speaking with the Almighty, face to face, and other similar expressions, we must look beyond the figurative style of the record, to the operation of *Divine power* upon the *minds* of men. Divine revelation is a plain and simple thing. It is not, as some suppose, limited in its operation, or confined to any single portion of mankind. It did not cease, as some assert, when the last Scripture-writer laid down his pen, but it continues to be manifested to us. We are the objects of our heavenly Father's regard. He has not only given us the light of the sun to illuminate the outward world, but he makes it to shine upon the evil and the good, the just and the unjust. And in the spiritual world there is the same universal diffusion of light that constitutes in the outward a monument of the benevolence of its Author. This light makes manifest to man the duties that are required of him, thus making the declaration of Paul true: "The grace of God that bringeth salvation hath appeared unto all men, teaching us that denying ungodliness and worldly lusts, we should live soberly, righteously, and godly in this present world." If we are prepared to subscribe to the doctrine that Divine grace hath appeared unto all men, and that it teaches them to deny all ungodliness, and live righteously in this present world, then we can understand, to what Jesus directed the attention of the people, and to what the ministry of the gospel should still direct them—*obedience to this light.* For just in proportion as we are obedient to it, we increase in the knowledge of the truth as it is in Jesus, "and go on adding to our faith virtue, to virtue knowledge, to knowledge patience, to patience temperance, to temperance godliness, to godliness brotherly kindness, to brotherly kindness charity." When we have gained all these then are we Christ-like; and the apostle says, if we continue to do these things we shall never fall, our knowledge of Christ will be saving, and an entrance gained into his "everlasting kingdom." Now, if the attention of the people was turned to the operation of Divine grace, implanted in their hearts, it would lead them step by step unto a knowledge of those things which pertain to the kingdom of heaven. It was because the Jews were not willing to rely upon the teaching of Divine grace, that Christ was rejected by them. Hence they persecuted and crucified Him who had been sent amongst them with the message of salvation. They were more attached to the traditions of men than the commandment of God. The simple truths of the gospel could meet with no favour while their reliance was upon a ceremonial and outward religion. The precepts of their law allowed "an eye for an eye, and a tooth for a tooth"—permitted them to "hate their enemies," and to return "evil for evil." They could practice their religion and still indulge the spirit of revenge and retaliation. But the precepts of the gospel inculcated directly to the opposite doctrine—the axe was to be laid at the root of the tree of evil; and a religious life was to consist in obedience to the Divine spirit and in love to man.

Now, my great concern is—and I desire to impress it upon our minds, that we may observe the injunction to watch and pray, lest we enter into temptation—that we may overcome the "lusts of the flesh, the lusts of the eye, and the pride of life"—and be able to say with the apostle, "There is now therefore no condemnation to them that are in Christ Jesus, who walk not after the flesh, but after the Spirit." What is this walking after the Spirit? We have an animal and a spiritual life, and as "one star differeth from another star in glory," so doth the greatness of the spiritual exceed the glory of the natural. The spiritual nature is that life which is "breathed into man and makes him a living soul. These tabernacles that compose the "terrestrial body" shall return again to dust. The spiritual nature constituting the "celestial body," is designed to live for ever. The great end of life can only be answered as this spiritual nature is prepared to enjoy the fountain from which it sprang. The beautiful design of the gospel is to elevate us above the earthly unto the heavenly nature—to give us the victory over the world, and prepare us for the society of sanctified spirits, not only now, but when time to us shall be no more. The gospel brings immortality to light, by putting us in possession of those treasures which "moth and rust cannot corrupt, or thieves break through and steal."

Let us then walk after the Spirit, in the light of this gospel, that when we are required to render an account of our stewardship we may be prepared to do it with the assurance of eternal union and communion with our Father in heaven. Let us examine the ground upon which we stand, and in what our religion consists. Let us examine our own minds, and see how far we have witnessed the Christ-like nature to govern us—to regulate our conduct—to preserve and save us from evil. Have we guarded "the avenues of the heart against the admission of evil?" Has the sin that doth so easily beset us been overcome and subdued? Are we conforming our lives to the example of Jesus? These are subjects that have an important bearing upon our present and future well-being. Let us seriously consider them. If we imitate the example of Jesus, our religion will be practical. Let us remember, that "if any man have not the spirit of Christ he is none of his;" and if we possess the "spirit of Christ," our minds will be clothed with love to God and our fellow-creatures; we shall fulfil the duties we owe to our Creator and one to another, and day by day we shall be engaged to "add to our faith virtue, to virtue knowledge, to knowledge patience, to patience temperance, to temperance godliness, to godliness brotherly kindness, and to brotherly kindness charity." And when we have made these heavenly attainments we shall be prepared to adopt as our own the language of Jesus:

"Father I have glorified thee on the earth, I have finished the work which thou gavest me to do."

[Here the speaker sat down, and in a short time rose and added:]

The language of the poet, "Know then thyself, enough for man to know," has been presented with instruction to my view. It is well for us to know ourselves; we may often derive encouragement and strength, by looking at the sources of good within our own minds. It is there the silent voice of truth is heard, and known and felt. And often this voice will be as a ministering spirit—an angel of light that will instruct and comfort us when all other sources of encouragement and comfort have failed. We need spiritual as well as physical strength, and as the latter is promoted by exercise, so will the former be increased by the proper employment of the gifts and talents we possess. It is thus that we shall become qualified to perform our mission of the gospel of Christ. What is this mission? If a brother or sister be overtaken with a fault, we should endeavour to restore such a one in the spirit of meekness and love, remembering ourselves lest we also be tempted. Our Christian duties often consist in little things, and it is a wise declaration, that "he that is faithful in a little shall be made ruler over more." By our obedience in little things we shall find that the field of duty and usefulness will enlarge, and we shall discover that there is no time for us to stand idle in the market-place, saying, "no man hath hired me." When we look around us we see the harvest is plenteous, while the labourers are few. In every work of religion, benevolence, and humanity, the call has gone forth, "enter into my vineyard and labour, and whatsoever is right ye shall receive." Time is swiftly drawing to a close, and it will soon be lost forever in the darkness of that night in which no man can work, and we are as fully convinced of this truth, that life must be followed by death, as we are of the change from day to night in the outward world. Some of us have reached the sixth, some the ninth, and some the eleventh hour; and it becomes a question of the greatest importance to us to know that we are so labouring in the Lord's vineyard as to realize our penny.

I feel the magnitude of the subject when I consider my own latter end. I am conscious that the present probation has its limits and they will soon be reached. I feel the necessity of faithfulness to truth and duty, and I desire above all things for myself and fellow-creatures, that we may make our "calling and election sure." I am satisfied, my friends, that if we live up to the knowledge that is received, the end of our being will be answered; we shall glorify God upon earth, enjoy his presence here and for ever. Oh, my friends, let us not be idle, but enter into the garden of our own minds and labour. There is a work there that is needful for us to perform—"man know thyself, enough for man to know." If we turn within ourselves we shall discover that the fountain of truth —of love—of light—is not far from any one of us. God is that fountain, and in him "we live and move, and have our being." Oh! blessed privilege, that we should have access to the source of all good, and have no more need that any man should instruct us in Divine things, than we have of trusting to others the salvation of our souls. The work of salvation belongs to us as individual heirs of immortality and eternal life, and it must be begun, carried on, and completed by our faithfulness and obedience to God. No man or woman ever performed an act of duty in accordance with the convictions of truth, who did not feel the reward of "well done, good and faithful servant." Well, my friends, if we have been rewarded for faithfulness in little things it should stimulate us to press forward towards the "mark for the prize of the high calling of God in Christ Jesus," and lead us to extend the invitation to others, to come and see how good the Lord is. Then should we be blessed by religious association, our spiritual strength would be renewed; the strong would encourage the weak, and when permitted to mingle with minds engaged in spiritual devotion, we should feel that we were in heavenly places in Christ Jesus, enjoying that unity of spirit on earth which shall bind the just of all generations together in the kingdom of heaven.

SERMON VII.

DELIVERED AT FRIENDS' MEETING, CHERRY STREET, PHILADELPHIA, IN THE EVENING OF FIRST MONTH 20TH, 1850.

"I AM not ashamed of the gospel of Christ, for it is the power of God unto salvation to every one that believeth."

I am a believer in the doctrine, that the gospel of Christ is "the power of God unto salvation," preached to every rational soul, in a manner so plain and intelligible, that all can understand it, and that the effects of obedience to its teachings, are the same in all ages of the world, and among all people, for it leads invariably to a life of devotion to God, and of usefulness to man. The great change that was effected in the conduct and experience of the apostle who made use of the expressions I have quoted, was produced according to his own testimony, when consulting not with flesh and blood, he gave up to the heavenly illuminations of truth upon his own mind, and was thus brought out of darkness into light, and from under the power and dominion of hatred and error, into the blessed liberty of the children of God. He could then say, "there is now, therefore, no condemnation to them that are in Christ Jesus, who walk not after the flesh, but after the spirit, for the law of the spirit of life in Christ Jesus hath set me free from the law of sin and death." The evident design of the gospel is to bring us into a state of blessedness, to lead us out of all error, into truth and righteousness. Since we have been together on the present occasion, this state, described by the apostle, as being without condemnation, has been presented to the view of my mind in such a light, that I have desired all in this assembly might see the beauty, simplicity and purity of the Christian's life, and desire to make it our's for its own eternal excellence, that we might realize the blessed enjoyment inseparable from continual obedience to the will of our Father who is in heaven. We bear the name of Christians among men, but the Christian religion does not consist in a name or profession of religion—not in word, but in deed—not in any cunningly devised fable, nor in every "wind of doctrine, and cunning craftiness of men, wherein they lie in wait to deceive," but in obedience to Christ. The Christian character so remarkable for its simplicity and purity, is easily distinguished from every thing of an opposite nature that has assumed its name. We have an infallible criterion by which it is to be known. When the blessed Jesus was engaged in the work of his mission, he told his disciples, that they should be judged by their fruits, and the rule is as applicable to us as to them. How simple is the test. "By their fruits ye shall know them; men do not gather grapes of thorns, or figs of thistles." The Christian is known by his fruits. "Not every one that saith unto me Lord, Lord, shall enter into the kingdom, but he that doeth the will of my Father which is in heaven," was another declaration of Jesus, pointing to the same thing, and showing that a profession to religion does not always imply that we have come to the kingdom of God.

Now, my friends, if I have any work to do in the gospel, it is not to be engaged in the defence of any of the speculative opinions, theories of religion, or systems of faith which have so unhappily led to strife and contention amongst men, but rather to bring before our view the practical and vital part of Christianity, to show us the necessity of daily obedience to Christ, that we may exhibit those fruits of righteousness by which the followers of Jesus will ever be known, and by which alone we can prove to others that we are "not ashamed of that gospel which is the power of God unto salvation, to every one that believeth." I consider it of no importance to make declarations of a belief in Christ, or in any thing else that pertains to religion, if our conduct does not correspond with our belief and profession; and yet we see how much dependence is placed upon a name to religion; how strenuously men are defending their opinions of Christ; their conflicting creeds and systems of faith; their forms and ceremonies, as though these constituted vital religion. Christ is not divided. It is in vain for us to say, "I am of Paul; and I of Apollos; and I of Cephas; and I of Christ." We have need to observe the command of Jesus—"If any man shall say unto you, lo, here is Christ, or there, believe it not, the kingdom of God is within you." The visible church has become scattered and divided amidst the conflict of opinions, and the strife of tongues which so unhappily prevail at the expense of practical and vital religion. Whatever we may profess, however beautiful may be our theory of religion, or however strictly we may observe external forms, if we neglect to fulfil the every-day duties of life, our cry of "Lord, Lord, open unto us," will be as ineffectual and unavailing as the cry of the foolish virgins in the parable, who had no oil in their vessels, and whose lamps had gone out. Now, my friends, I consider there is no subject of so much importance to us as that of religion, rightly understood and carried out in practice. Our present and eternal well-being is involved in it. But it consists not in a name —not in a belief in any system of faith—not in the observance of any form; it is beautifully described by the Apostle James in these words: "Pure religion, and undefiled before God and the Father, is this, to visit the fatherless and the widows in their affliction, and to keep himself unspotted from the world."

Religion becomes practical and useful, or theoretical and speculative, according to the standard we adopt, by which the truth of all doctrines and principles regulating human conduct is to be tested; and whatever difference of opinion may exist on this subject, one thing is certain, that if we take the example of Jesus as the standard, for the "perfect and upright man," there can be no misunderstanding as to what the primary obligations of religion are, for none will deny that he was continually engaged in doing the will of his heavenly Father; in proving his love to God, by doing good to man. The work of his mission was clearly defined when he entered the synagogue and read these words from the book of the prophet Esaias: "The spirit of the Lord is upon me, because he hath anointed me to preach the gospel to the poor; he hath sent me to heal the broken-hearted; to preach deliverance to the captives, and recovering of sight to the blind; to set at liberty them that are bruised; to preach the acceptable year of the Lord." Is the life and example of Jesus made the standard of the popular religion of our day? I believe not. The standard is in opinion rather than practice. In professions of faith rather than works. There are great efforts made to set up written tests of sound doctrine, to call the people more to an opinionative and speculative religion than to practical righteousness, and hence a great deal of the profession of religion is but "as sounding brass and a tinkling cymbal." What has been gained by calling men to creeds and theories of religion, or even to those writings to which we give the appellation of Scriptures of Truth? If we are to judge the state of the Christian church by the fruits that have been exhibited, this practice has not promoted that harmony and charity which are indispensable to the Christian character. Almost every sect in Christendom call the Scriptures their rule of faith and practice, they look to them as the highest oracle of truth, and many go so far as to style them the infallible word of God; and yet it is an undeniable truth, that there is as wide a difference among them as there is between Jew and Christian, Pagan and Mahometan. Let us look for the proof of this to the scenes of strife and contention, the bigotry and intolerance that have been manifested by sect towards sect, and we shall see with all this professed reverence for the Scriptures, there is a great want of that fundamental principle of which the blessed Jesus spoke when he said, "By this shall all men know that ye are my disciples if ye have love one to another." How sad is the retrospect of the past, and how much to be regretted the present divided state of Christians. The warrior does not display more bitterness of spirit in the field of carnage than is often manifested by these towards each other, and yet the persecuted and the persecutors alike go to the Scriptures to establish their respective creeds and systems of faith. Influenced by a blind and superstitious veneration for the letter, men have conceived that others must necessarily understand it as themselves, and from this cause thousands of martyrs, whose lives have been spotless in the sight of heaven, have been required to seal their testimony with their blood. A slight difference of opinion in the interpretations of Scripture has given rise to angry controversy and sectarian prejudice, that have not unfrequently led the disputants into the field of slaughter, where they have committed the deplorable folly of testing the orthodoxy of their creeds by the victories of battle. Now we see that harmony and love, becoming the followers of Christ, does not abound among those who say that the Scriptures are their rule of faith and practice, neither has the church been "brought out of the wilderness of lifeless forms and ceremonies to lean on the bosom of its beloved." It is not only in reference to abstract doctrines and opinions that this diversity of view exists, but also upon some of the plainest questions of righteousness and morality, there is a wide difference of opinion or understanding of Scripture. Thus we find that monstrous violation of human rights which dooms to hopeless servitude millions of our fellow-men, and places them on a level with the beasts of the field, is attempted to be defended as a Divine institution by the authority of Scripture. By many the Bible is appealed to in order to prove that wars and fightings, and even the indiscriminate massacre of an entire nation of people, has been carried on by positive Divine command, and that the barbarous custom of inflicting the punishment of death is an institution of Jehovah, binding upon the present, as well as upon past generations of men. Now, while the Scriptures admit of such various and contradictory interpretations—while there continues to be so much controversy with regard to their meaning—while no two sects can comprehend them alike, it proves, with the clearness of a moral demonstration, that they do not come up to the standard of a rule so plain, that the "way-faring man, though a fool, cannot misunderstand it;" and, therefore they are not an adequate rule, nor the primary standard of faith and practice, which would be plain and self-evident. There is a higher standard of faith and practice than the Scriptures. It is comprehended in the words of Jesus, to which I have already alluded—"By their fruits ye shall know them." The most certain test of sound doctrine, is a sound life—a holy life—a life in which all the Christian virtues are daily exhibited. How true is the expression of the poet:—

"For modes of faith let graceless zealots fight,
His can't be wrong whose life is in the right."

It is a doctrine universally true and self-evident, that if the fruit be good, the tree that produces it must be good also; and no sophistry of man, no fine spun theory of religion, can alter or amend an infallible criterion like this. It was in agreement with this great natural and universal truth that Jesus gave his precept; and until the religious world adopt this as the standard by which the value of all doctrines of religion or morality shall be estimated—until they come to judge of men's fitness for heaven, by the fruits of their lives and not by their creeds, there will continue to be the same confusion of language and strife of tongues—the same sectarian animosity that has, in times past, and still continues to "divide in Jacob and scatter Israel."

Perhaps some will say, that in making these remarks, I am undervaluing the Scriptures and making them of no account—I think otherwise. Upon this subject it seems right that I should further enlarge. I desire not to be misunderstood. I have loved to read the Scriptures from my childhood up to the present hour; some of the earliest religious impressions that memory can recall, accompanied the perusal of the experience of the righteous that is there recorded. I recur now to an incident connected with my earliest religious convictions, so memorable to me, that it will be lasting as life itself, in which my mind in the infancy of experience was led to feel and admire the truth of some of these Scripture declarations. I had learned to repeat that beautiful prayer which Jesus taught his disciples, and often to open my lips with the language, "Our Father, who art in heaven." In the spirit of inquiry natural to childhood, I was led on one of those occasions of retirement, that I had been taught was necessary to effectual prayer, to put this question to myself, what good can it do me to repeat these words, or how shall I be benefited by the use of this prayer? I was seeking after truth, and in the silence that followed the inquiry, my understanding was addressed by a language like this—The value of thy prayer depends upon the spirit in which it is made. Oh, the impressions of that hour have followed me through life, and I shall carry the remembrance thereof with me to the grave; and I wish I could convey to others the convictions I have received myself, that however much we may read the Scriptures, or repeat the declarations of good men that we find there recorded, they can be of no value to us, only as we are brought into a state of mind in which we can make those declarations our's. Then only can we say with truth, "Our Father, who art in heaven, hallowed be thy name; thy kingdom come, thy will be done on earth, as it is done in heaven." I say then, I have loved the Scriptures from my childhood. The truths contained in them I have ever held in high esteem. For fifteen years I have laboured in this vineyard, and I know not that I have ever been called to speak in the assemblies of the people but it has been my lot to refer to the testimonies of Scripture, while engaged in the work of the ministry; and whenever I have quoted them, it has been from a conviction of their truth. If this is not evidence of my regard for the Scriptures I need offer no other.

But while I have read with instruction and encouragement the many declarations of truth which they contain, I cannot call the Bible the word of God; I cannot look to it as the highest oracle of truth, for I believe the immediate and inward teaching of the Holy Spirit is as much above any of the writings of men as the heavens are higher than the earth.

The Bible was written by men, and like every other human work, it is liable to imperfection and error, and I believe that those who are undertaking to prove that every thing which is contained within its lids is a Divine revelation, are doing the Scriptures and the cause of truth more harm than all the open infidelity with which they have ever been assailed. We are commanded to "try the spirits;" we must try the "letter" also, by the light of truth in our own minds, which is "Christ in you the hope of glory." When we come to be taught by him we shall have our spiritual vision opened, and be able to discriminate between that which is written by inspiration of God, and that which has proceeded from the commandments and traditions of men. The Scriptures do not point to themselves as a sufficient rule of life, but they tell us to "*mark the perfect man*, and behold the upright, for the end of that man is peace." How true is this declaration—the end of the perfect and the upright man is peace—peace with God, and peace with all men, it is the highest state of excellence to which in the present life we can attain.

Oh, my brethren, let me ask you to consider the importance of this distinguishing virtue and uprightness. It is this that gives true dignity and honour to human conduct, it lies at the very foundation of a moral and religious reputation, and if we fail to carry it out in our intercourse with each other, we can never maintain an unblemished life among men. Uprightness leads to strict integrity, justice, and the love of truth, in all the common affairs of life. The religion of the "perfect and the upright man" is for every day. It is not to be put off and on like a garment. It is blended with all our intercourse with the world, and will so regulate our conduct, that we shall never sacrifice our integrity for the love of gain. I fear we are not sufficiently guarded on this subject. I wish we may keep the eye single to the truth, and carry out to the very letter that admirable precept of Jesus, "Whatsoever ye would that men should do unto you, do ye even so to them." If the principle of uprightness were carried out in all the concerns of life, what examples of honesty would be seen on every hand; we could do no wrong to our fellow-men, for we should see that the deceiver was in the spirit of anti-Christ, and that to practice deception, is to "crucify afresh the Son of God, and put him to open shame." Now when I consider the character of the "perfect and the upright man," when I reflect that honesty, justice and uprightness, constitute the certain path to happiness and peace, it appears to me to be a mark of short-sightedness—a want of true wisdom on our part to neglect those duties, and by so doing, barter away an inheritance infinitely more valuable than all the treasures and honours this world can afford.

Time, my friends, is swiftly passing away, and to us it will soon be no more; we are rapidly following those who have gone before us to the house appointed for the living, and thus we have the timely admonition that here we have "no continuing city;" that the present is not our final home; that death is inevitable, and the eternal future near at hand. Should not these reflections stir up the pure mind in us, to contemplate with seriousness the great design of life, the obligations we are under to the Author of our Being, and the duties we owe to each other as children of one common Father. We should not be discouraged thereby, but stimulated to improve our time, to apply our hearts to wisdom, to remember our latter end. What value do we set on time? It is an inestimable treasure, a sacred trust committed to our care. Shall we squander it away, and torture our existence by abuse and by folly? No. Let us improve it to the glory of God, and our own good. Cultivate the garden of our own minds. We have many gifts and talents bestowed upon us by a benevolent Creator, and they are intended to be improved, that the soul may be expanded and prepared to enjoy the infinite Fountain from which it sprang. Among these endowments of the Creator, is included our intellectual nature, which is as much a gift of God, as the gift of grace, and we are as responsible for the culture and improvement of the one, as of the other. I have no idea that such a noble talent is to be buried in the earth, that it is to be employed merely in procuring food and raiment for these frail temples which are soon to moulder in the dust. Far otherwise. There is a beautiful relation between mind and matter, between the works of God, and our capacity to contemplate them. "The heavens declare the glory of God, and the firmament showeth his handy work." We need not go after fiction, for every page of the great volume of nature is full of living and instructive truth. Placed in the midst of a beautiful creation, we are invited to meditate on the workmanship of its Author, and such an exercise of the intellect is profitable to us, for it leads to humility, and while it makes manifest the feebleness of man, exalts our views of the wisdom, goodness, and power of the Creator, and shows us that order is "heaven's first law." The study of nature is not incompatible with true devotion to God. The right improvement of the spiritual and intellectual gifts bestowed upon us by the Giver of all good, will lead into the same train of reflections that called forth this acknowledgment from a Christian philosopher: "O thou, who by the light of nature, dost kindle in us a desire after the light of grace, that by it we may reach the light of thy glory; I give thee thanks, O Lord and Creator, that thou hast gladdened me by thy Creation, when I was enraptured by the work of thy hands." It will enable us to adopt the sentiment of the Psalmist: "When I consider thy heavens, the work of thy fingers, the moon and the stars which thou hast ordained; what is man that thou art mindful of him, and the Son-of-man that thou visitest him?" And when we are thus humbled by the contemplation of our comparative nothingness, amidst the immensity of creation, we shall learn what constitutes the true greatness of man. " Thou hast made him a little lower than the angels, and hast crowned him with glory and honour. Thou madest him to have dominion over the works of thy hands: thou hast put all things under his feet. O Lord, our Lord, how excellent is thy name in all the earth!"

Here is portrayed the final destiny of man. "Thou hast crowned him with glory and honour." Thus opening to his view the sublime doctrine of the soul's immortality, and the joys and prospects that stand connected with an eternal world.

Oh, my friends, we are invited to lay hold of this crown of life, which is the reward of the perfect and the upright man. Let us keep this great object of our being in view, follow the example of Jesus, seek after inward and spiritual communion with the Infinite Mind, that we may be rightly instructed in the duties of life; and as we are obedient to all the revealings of Divine truth, we shall be governed by the same rule, and mind the same thing that has enabled the righteous of past ages to walk with God; and we also shall be numbered at last with the just of all generations, made perfect in the kingdom of heaven.

" God, thus to thee our lowly thoughts shall soar,
Thus seek thy presence, Being, wise and good
'Midst thy vast works; admire, obey, adore,
And when the tongue is eloquent no more,
The soul shall speak in tears of gratitude."

SERMON VIII.

DELIVERED AT FRIENDS' MEETING, GREEN STREET, PHILADELPHIA, THIRD MONTH 10TH, 1850.

If the records of the past may be taken in evidence, I think we have a right to infer that mankind have always been disposed to the reverence of a superior power; for it does not appear on the pages of history that there ever was a time, since the creation of man, when the acknowledgment of a belief in the existence of a Supreme Governor of the universe, and of man's accountability to him for his course of conduct, was not made: and so far as our knowledge of the present inhabitants of the globe has extended, this view is confirmed; for we have an evidence, even among those nations who are sunk to the greatest degree in ignorance and idolatry, that all traces of this belief have not waned into total extinction. It is no argument against the universality of such a conviction, that this simple belief has been embarrassed and encumbered by false notions and opinions concerning the Divine character—the relation that exists between man and his Maker—and the duties and obligations that the creature owes to the Creator. For, although in the darkness of the human understanding, it has been burdened with false notions of the adoration which is his due—with senseless forms and ceremonies which have been founded in superstition, and have led to all manner of idolatry and error, still there are evidences that from the human mind this conviction of the existence of a Supreme Being has not been wholly eradicated.

It would seem to be impossible to account for the universality of this belief, unless we adopt a view which is abundantly illustrated in the Scriptures, confirmed and enforced by the testimony of human experience in all ages, that it is the "same God that worketh all in all," who giveth "a manifestation of the spirit to every man to profit withal." The same view is represented as a law written upon the heart, so effectual and sufficient of itself, to give man a knowledge of his Creator, that it is positively declared, "they shall teach no more every man his neighbour, nor every man his brother, saying, know the Lord; for all shall know me from the least of them unto the greatest of them, saith the Lord."

There is abundant testimony of this kind, left upon record in the Scriptures and other writings, from which we draw the conclusion that Divine goodness has not left himself without a witness, but that he has communicated a knowledge of his own being and nature to all men of every kindred, nation, tongue and people, so effectually, as to make the declaration of the apostle true, where he says, "Ye have an unction from the Holy One, and ye know all things;" "the anointing which ye have received of him abideth in you, and ye need not that any man teach you; but as the same anointing teacheth you of all things, and is truth and is no lie." This "manifestation of the spirit"—this "law written on the heart"—this "unction" and "anointing" which ye have received, is, to use another Scripture expression, the "true light that lighteth *every man* that cometh into the world," and is what we understand to be, immediate, Divine revelation. It is the Deity revealing himself to man, and it ever has been, and still continues to be, a universal illumination that embraces the whole of his rational, intelligent creation. I am aware there are many who call this in question, and who presume to deny the immediate intercourse between the soul and its author; there are those who assert that immediate, Divine revelation does not now exist—that the period has passed by when it was consistent with the Infinite Jehovah to unfold immediately to his accountable children the knowledge of himself, and his will concerning them, by opening before them the way in which they should go. Let us examine and consider in what this revelation consists. Let us open the great volume of our own experience, and read attentively the record made upon our own minds, and we shall find that so far as it relates to ourselves individually, there has been a Divine revelation to us, and that this has been repeated, day by day, and hour by hour.

It was the declaration of the apostle James, that "every good gift and every perfect gift is from above, and cometh down from the Father of lights, with whom there is neither variableness, neither shadow of turning." Every impression of Divine truth that man receives, proceeds from our Father in heaven, and it is as certainly a Divine revelation to him as any opening or manifestation of truth that was ever made to any Patriarch, Prophet, or Apostle that has gone before him; and he knows perfectly well, as he reads this law written on the heart, that his happiness—his hope of heaven depends upon his obedience to the light of truth in his own mind. So far from this Divine revelation having ceased, it continues to impress upon the human soul the image of its author; to give man a knowledge of God; to open to all the way in which they should go; and all who obey its teachings—who carry out in the practice of life the duties it requires of them, are found fearing God and working righteousness; and whatever their name to religion may be, whether Jew or Greek, Pagan or Christian, they belong to the church of Christ on earth, and will be numbered at last with the "general assembly and church of the first born which are written in heaven."

Now, it is because men have forsaken this fountain of living instruction, through which a true knowledge of the Divine nature is communicated, that their systems of religion have become obscured with absurd opinions and speculations, and their minds become darkened by perverted views of the Deity and of the nature of the homage which is his due. Thus darkness has spread in the earth—the church has gone into the wilderness—where, instead of that order, harmony and peace, which is typical of the kingdom of heaven and the Church of Christ, mystery, confusion and discord are seen on every side; and so long as religion is made to consist in embracing the views and opinions of others—more than in obedience to those convictions of truth in our minds, this confusion and strife will always continue. We do not sufficiently consider the relation in which we stand to the author of our being; for, if the Scripture declaration is true, (and I cannot doubt it) "they shall teach no more every man his neighbour, and every man his brother, saying, know the Lord: for they shall all know me, from the least of them to the greatest of them," why is it not relied on in practice? why shall man lean upon his fellow; or be looking to the opinions of others for a knowledge of God and his truth?

Having access to the fountain itself, why shall we give up to the keeping and control of others that immortal spirit which the Creator has bestowed upon us? We should consider ourselves responsible for the proper use and exercise of *all* the gifts and blessings which we have received. Man inherits from his Maker the gift of conscience; its exercise embraces the right of private judgment in all matters pertaining to his spiritual well being. In the exercise of this right, we may try by the light of truth upon our own understanding, all doctrines, opinions, and theories of religion that are offered to our acceptance; and if they do not accord with the convictions of truth upon our own minds, we are at liberty to reject them—yes, we are bound to reject them, or else we are making a false and dangerous use of the gifts that have been bestowed upon us. When the human mind forsakes the only infallible teacher, and submits to be enslaved by the opinions of men, it is constantly in danger of surrendering the inestimable rights of conscience and of judgment, and becoming darkened by strange and benighted views of the Divine character, is led into a multitude of useless forms and observances, and even into the grossest idolatry. These causes have operated unfavourably to human progress, and have greatly contributed to the spread of an erroneous theology, which has kept man groping his way in darkness, a stranger to the road on which he is traveling, and ignorant of the destiny that awaits him at the end of his journey; but, by obedience to these simple revelations, man is led out of darkness and error into light and truth, and from under the dominion and power of evil into the liberty of the children of God.

Many are taught by their teachers of religion, that they are to receive the knowledge of the truth from men, or from the Scriptures,—the "letter" that "killeth," is placed above the "spirit that giveth life;" and thus the mind is drawn away from its own convictions of truth to a dependence upon the opinions and teachings of men. "Ye need not that any man teach you;" we are not dependent on man or upon books, however good they may be, for Divine truth is communicated without their instrumentality.

I am reminded of the testimony given by an Indian, which I heard in this house some years ago, when relating the experience of his early life; he declared, that before he came within the pale of human civilization, before he had ever heard the name of Jesus, or known the Scriptures, he felt and knew the operation of the Holy Spirit; he was conversant with the voice of truth in his own breast, and to his great astonishment when he came to read the experience of others as recorded in the Scriptures, he found it ran parallel with his own, and that other minds had also felt the same impressions of goodness and truth, leading them to love God, and to do good to man. Were not these Divine revelations? I have heard the Mahometan, devotedly attached to the religion of his fathers, declare it as his firm and unshaken faith that all men of every nation upon the earth received immediately from the author of their being, impressions of divine good. These impressions are Divine revelations. The popular opinion maintains that all those who have not the Bible are in a state of alienation from God, and doomed to eternal perdition. This view is held up by some of the high professors of Christianity, who seem to think that if they can only send the Bible to the heathen, and get them to subscribe to their creeds and opinions, that their salvation will be secured. Thus the cry of "I am of Paul, I of Apollos, I of Cephas, or I am of Christ," has gone forth into all lands, professedly for the recovery of our benighted fellow-creatures from idolatry to the true worship of God. Let us look at the inconsistency, if not the insincerity, of these professions for a moment. Do we suppose that even these are so totally depraved and wrapped in moral darkness, as to have the light of heaven entirely shut out from them? Do we judge them on account of their idolatry, and say that every good and virtuous emotion has been obliterated? When we contemplate them standing around their sacrifices and witnessing with delight the dying agonies of their human victims, or offering their children to idols, shall we say that not a single ray of Divine truth has ever penetrated their dark and benighted state? Let us look upon the other side of the picture; and our views perhaps will be modified by what we find countenanced and encouraged by that portion of mankind who enjoy the blessings of civilization, who are conversant with the writings of the Scriptures, and are acquainted with the example and precepts of Jesus as there recorded. We find those who are professing the Christian name, and claiming to be the "lights of the world," guilty of crimes as enormous in the sight of heaven as those of the poor ignorant heathen, when he offers his children to idols. Look at the many thousands of human sacrifices that the professors of the religion of Jesus are offering to the god of war, in the unbounded indulgence of passion—at the promptings of worldly ambition and revenge. Might not the heathen with equal propriety retort upon us and say, these Christians are without a single ray of Divine truth, or they never would be guilty of so much cruelty. While professing Christians are offering their thousands and tens of thousands of human sacrifices to the god of war, they have little room to accuse the heathen of idolatry and wickedness. For the day will come when their conduct will be viewed by a more enlightened and righteous posterity, with the same feelings of abhorrence that we now look upon that portion of mankind whom we are seeking to reclaim from the moral darkness, ignorance and superstition by which they are surrounded. I know that this declaration cannot be verified till after the lapse of ages, and the testimony of generations that are yet unborn; but I am unshaken in the belief, that when clear and enlightened views of the Divine character prevail,—when man comes to see the true relation in which he stands to his Creator and to his fellow,—when the mists of darkness and error that now envelop the minds of men shall be dispelled by the light of the sun of righteousness, then war and all its kindred evils of violence, oppression and wrong will be banished from the earth forever.

Herein is an inconsistency apparent—that we should manifest so much zeal for the conversion of others to Christianity—and yet leave untouched and unrebuked the vices of Christians themselves.

What should Christians be? "Ye are the light of the world," said the blessed Jesus: "A city that is set on a hill cannot be hid." "Let your light so shine before men that they may see your good works and glorify your Father which is in heaven." We claim to have Christ for our teacher and our example; but this profession is of itself of no value, when we consider that it is said, "Not every one that saith unto me Lord, Lord, shall enter into the kingdom of heaven; but he that doeth the will of my Father which is in heaven."

The credit and honour of a profession to serve Christ, is to carry out in the daily practice of life the precepts and doctrines of the gospel. Religion does not consist in a name, nor are its duties fulfilled by subscribing to systems of faith, and to opinions of men; neither does it consist in the observance of forms and ceremonies, but in doing the will of our Father who is in heaven. I have said this will is manifested within us—it is revealed by the voice of truth to the soul. And to what does it lead? It never led any man to hate his brother. It teaches us to love, not to hate: always to do good, never to do evil. Jesus defined the nature of its instructions and promptings in the command, "Love your enemies, bless them that curse you, do good to them that hate you, and pray for them that despitefully use you and persecute you; that ye may be the children of your Father which is in heaven: for he maketh his sun to rise on the evil and on the good, and sendeth rain on the just and on the unjust."

This, my friends, is practical Christianity. If we would reform mankind—if we would become instruments in gathering others into the fold of Christ—it cannot be done by preaching or by circulating the Scriptures. We must become by our example, "the light of the world," we must so live in the practice of righteousness, that "others seeing our *good works*, may glorify our Father in heaven."

I desire therefore that our minds may be fully impressed with the conviction, that pure religion consists in fulfilling all the duties and obligations of life that devolve upon us, as believers in the existence of a Supreme Being to whom we are accountable, and as followers of Jesus Christ.

Are there any who can doubt the existence of an All-wise Creator? "The fool hath said in his heart, there is no God." I know there are those who attempt by the light of reason to shut out the Creator from the universe, and to disclaim his superintendence in the government of the world. Let us examine this for a moment, and we shall perceive that it is the "fool" only "who hath said in his heart there is no God."

All the deductions of reason are susceptible of proof. Every conclusion that the human mind arrives at by a process of reasoning, must be sustained by adequate evidence. If we would prove, by the light of reason, that there is no God, we must first show that there is no evidence of design—no indications of skill—contrivance, or adaption of means to ends, in the visible universe: for the moment we admit the evidence of these, or fail to show that they do not exist, we admit at once the certainty of an Intelligent Mind, for we cannot conceive of the existence of the one without the other. Well, now, if thou would show by reason that there is not an Intelligent Creator, let me ask thee, to prove that the *eye* was not made for *seeing*, or the *ear* for hearing. By what process of reason canst thou reach the conclusion that the organ of vision was not adapted to the nature of light, or that the ear was not constructed in agreement with the laws of sound? Follow up the order of nature from the meanest reptile, to that being who is created but "little lower than the angels, and crowned with glory and honour," and thou will find innumerable traces of an Infinite, Intelligent Mind, manifested by proofs of design, contrivance, adaptation and skill, which thy reason will not permit thee to evade or deny. Again, follow up the chain of the material creation, from the grain of sand on the sea shore, to the contemplation of countless worlds, that are distributed over the regions of space, and thou wilt see that order prevails throughout every department of nature; that everything is governed by its appropriate law. Can law exist without a Lawgiver? Can order, harmony and skill result from any other than an Intelligent source? No, never. Use thy reason rightly, and it will convince thee, that without a Creator, creation, with its proofs of design, could not have existed, and that without the continual exercise of creative power, the present order of nature could not for a moment continue. Here then we shall find that the attempt to reason the Deity out of the universe, is to *abuse* this noble gift; while its proper exercise and deductions lead us to the same conclusion that the Apostle arrived at, when he said, "The invisible things of him from the creation of the world are clearly seen, being understood by the things that are made, even his eternal power and Godhead; so that they are without excuse." Leaving then those proofs of the existence of a Creator, inscribed upon all his works, and which the light of reason unfolds, let us turn the attention of him that doubts, to that which is passing within his own breast. Whence is that moral responsibility, that attaches itself to every part of human conduct? Why do we know and feel the distinction between right and wrong, truth and error? It is because we are accountable beings, and have a measure of this light "that lighteth every man that cometh into the world." This that I first alluded to, as being sufficient to give us a true knowledge of the Creator, and of the duties and obligations that we owe to him, and to our fellow-creatures. This light is not of man, but of God.

Here our mission must end. We can commend one another to "God and the word of his grace, which is able to build you up, and to give you an inheritance among all them which are sanctified." We can direct one another to those convictions of truth, by which the understanding may be opened to comprehend the purity and eternal excellence of the Divine nature, and the soul led step by step to realize the joys of heaven. We are progressive beings. Progression and development are laws of our being. It is true in the natural, and it is no less true in the spiritual world. The Apostle defined this when he says, "We know in part, we prophesy in part; but when that which is perfect is come, that which is in part shall be done away. When I was a child, I thought as a child, I spake as a child, I understood as a child; but when I became a man I put away childish things." Now this is true in a spiritual sense. It is little by little that our minds become enlarged to see the beauty and truth of the religion of Jesus, and to experience the blessings that are inseparably connected with the practice thereof. What was the language of Jesus? "Blessed are the meek, for they shall inherit the earth. Blessed are the merciful, for they shall obtain mercy. Blessed are the pure in heart, for they shall see God. Blessed are the peacemakers, for they shall be called the children of God." Do we not see that we can never enjoy these blessings, till we come into the possession of these heavenly virtues? Are not meekness, purity, mercy, peace, angels of light sent forth to minister to all them who are heirs of salvation; and does not the presence of these, and similar powers, destroy their opposites in the soul? The angel of love overcomes the devil of hatred, the light of justice warns us against all injustice, mercy preserves us from cruelty, humility subdues pride, and the angel of hope overcomes the demon of despair. As these gain the ascendency in the soul, we become Christ-like, and are made partakers of a heavenly kingdom.

This is the religion of Jesus. These are the *states* of which he spoke when he said, "In my father's house are many mansions; if it were not so, I would have told you; I go to prepare a place for you, that where I am, there ye may be also." Jesus is our example. Let us follow him through all these mansions of meekness, humility, love, kindness, charity—these are the *works* which he did, and which we also are called to do.

Let us not presume that we have reached a point, beyond which there is no further progress in the knowledge of the truth or divine things. Jesus declared to the people of his time: "I have many things to say unto you, but ye cannot bear them now." It is an error into which many of the professors of religion have fallen, that after they have subscribed to certain opinions, and adopted the doctrines and speculations of their creeds, to think they have arrived at a full knowledge of the truth; and claiming that they only are right, are often ready to condemn, and would persecute even unto death, those who may differ from them in opinion.

The Bible in the hands of these, instead of being an instrument to gather to the Church of Christ, or used to promote a religion that consists in "visiting the widow and the fatherless in their afflictions, and keeping ourselves unspotted from the world," is employed to divide Christendom into sects and parties, and to make matters of religion a bone of contention. If religion was made to consist in the practice of righteousness, and not in speculations and opinions; in being good and doing good, and not in subscribing to any written creed, there could be none of those controversies about it, that separate man from his brother. It is to be hoped that the day will come, when the simple and beautiful religion of Jesus, will be carried more into practice, and be a restraint upon the conduct and actions of men, in the various callings of every day life. I have no faith whatever in confining the duties of religion to the observance of days and times. This is not sufficient to answer the purpose for which we profess to worship the Creator. We must carry out its principles in every day life, and prove that we are Christians, by fulfilling all life's duties. We must treat our fellow-beings as brethren —the children of a common father, created for the same great purpose, and bound to the same eternity. We should not consider that when these bodies shall return to the dust, that it is the end of our being, but we should contemplate life with those enlarged views, that embrace the future as well as the present state; and recognizing in each other the birth of an immortal mind, endeavour to cultivate and secure a unity of spirit, that shall render us happier here, and continue to be a blessing when time shall be no more.

I would ask thee, my brother or my sister, to examine these things for thyself. Go not after the cry of "I am of Paul, I am of Apollos, I am of Cephas, or I am of Christ;" which is drawing thy attention to men and to books, rather than to the law of God written in thy heart. Read the volume of thy own experience. What is the sin that doth easily beset thee? In what respect art thou most in danger of falling? What is thy greatest temptation? I ask thee, to watch at that point with increasing vigilance. The sin that doth easily beset thee may be removed, and watchfulness will be thy preservation in the hour of temptation and trial. The language of the beloved of God, is addressed to thee: "What I say unto one I say unto all, watch! watch and pray, and that continually, lest ye enter into temptation."

It is by watchfulness and prayer that we are able to resist and overcome one temptation after another; strength will be given us to regulate and subdue every propensity and passion, that may have controlled our better nature; thus, day by day, we may gain the victory over the world, and be prepared to enjoy the true communion of Christ: "To him that overcometh will I give to sit with me on my throne, even as I have overcome and am set down with my father on his throne."

This is the reward of our faithfulness to truth and duty; as we are obedient to all the revealings of light and knowledge, we shall feel the reward of our stewardship to be peace, when in the solemn hour that is not far distant, this language shall be addressed to us, "Set thy house in order, for thou shalt die and not live." What is death to him that has overcome the world? Such a mind need not contemplate eternity with fear or gloom; for if we can taste and handle of the "good word of life and the powers of the world to come," death will be disarmed of its sting—the grave will have no victory, and we shall look forward to the future world, with the blessed assurance of an inheritance in that city, whose inhabitants cannot say, "I am sick."

Let me impress upon your minds the necessity of giving "all diligence to make our calling and election sure," by fulfilling the design of our being, in accomplishing the work that has been given us to do. O, dear young people, there is nothing of so much importance to your present and future peace, and the highest interests that can concern you are involved in the labour, that you should shape your course of life, in agreement with the beautiful religion of Jesus. There is nothing that can bless you, or make life to you so much a scene of enjoyment, as to follow the example of him who said, "Suffer little children to come unto me and forbid them not, for of such is the kingdom of heaven." Turn your thoughts to God; cultivate the love of virtue, purity and truth. Avoid the evils—the snares, and the vices that are around you: for this purpose, there is strength given to you, and if you make not use of the power that is thus bestowed upon you, the day may come when the dangers to which you are exposed will overcome you, and you may have to adopt the language that one did of old: "Oh that I were as in months past, as in the day when God preserved me; when his candle shined upon my head, and when by his light I walked through darkness."

I believe there are those present, whose minds have been visited with powerful convictions of truth;

and if these are obedient to these heavenly visions, they will become as lights to the world, and as instruments in the Divine hand, in calling others to behold the beauty of the truth as it is in Jesus. I would say to these, leave the things that are behind; "go on unto perfection;" keep the eye single to the light of truth, and He who has called you by his power will not only be to you as the light of the morning, but he will be your meridian and your evening sun. It is not my mission to turn your attention to men, or to the opinions and speculations of men: "For ye are not come unto the mount that might be touched, and that burned with fire, nor unto blackness, and darkness and tempest, and to the sound of the trumpet, and the voice of words! But ye are called unto Mount Zion, and unto the city of the living God, the heavenly Jerusalem, and to an innumerable company of angels, to the general assembly and church of the first-born which are written in heaven, and to God the Judge of all, and to the spirits of just men made perfect."

It is my concern to invite all, and especially my young friends, to a just and serious contemplation of the duties of life. Our happiness depends upon the fulfilment of these duties. Let us keep in view that pure and heavenly state, represented under the figure of the "holy city, new Jerusalem, coming down from God out of heaven, prepared as a bride adorned for her husband." The more we contemplate this state, and seek to make it ours, the more we shall be led to see and admire the wisdom, love, mercy and goodness of our father in heaven; and as we rightly consider the relation in which we stand to him as the author of our being, and our dependence upon his guidance to lead us safely amidst all the temptations and trials incident to our present course of probation, the reflection and acknowledgement of the poet will be ours:

> "Thou art the source and centre of all minds,
> Their only point of rest, eternal Word!
> From thee departing, they are lost, and rove
> At random, without honour, hope, or peace."

SERMON IX.

DELIVERED AT FRIENDS' MEETING, DARBY, NINTH MONTH 22D, 1850.

It appears from the testimony left upon record, that the great example and teacher we profess to follow, in the course of his ministry, called the attention of the people to the observance of a higher and purer morality than was recognized by the religion of that day. He proclaimed the truth of God, in opposition to the prejudices and traditions in which they were educated, and called them away from the inferior morality of the law to the benign and heavenly influences of the gospel. This, I think, is evident, if we believe his precepts. "Ye have been told," he says, "by them of old time, thou shalt love thy neighbour and hate thine enemy." This was the rule by which the conduct of man towards his fellow-man was regulated. A morality that encouraged *hatred,* or any other disposition so entirely foreign to the loveliness of God, could not be passed unnoticed by the blessed Jesus; and hence, at the commencement of his mission of love and mercy, he called their attention to it, and added, "I say unto you, *love your enemies;* do good to them that hate you; bless them that curse you, and pray for them that persecute you and despitefully use you." He also gave them many other precepts in relation to human duty and conduct which might be referred to in illustration of the fact, that he preached a higher and purer doctrine than was practised by the Jews. These principles of action, laid down by Jesus, form the basis of true morality, and obedience to them the starting point in religion.

The object of Christianity is unquestionably to eradicate all evil from the society of men; to bring down heaven upon earth; to lay the axe at the root of the tree of error, that it may destroy its fruits; to change the condition of man from the image of the earthly to the heavenly nature, and elevate him in the scale of spiritual progression in the knowledge of the attributes of God.

In advancing this great doctrine of loving our enemies and doing good to them that hate us, Jesus gave a very clear and powerful argument in its favour; he had a reason for the hope that was in him, and it is worthy of our notice, that all doctrine pertaining to the welfare of the soul must be addressed to our rational perception, and contain in itself some recommendation of its usefulness to man. When, therefore, he urged them to love their enemies, and return good instead of evil for evil, he gave them this reason: "That you may be the children of your Father which is in heaven; for he maketh his sun to rise on the evil and on the good, and sendeth rain on the just and on the unjust. For if ye love them which love you, what reward have ye? Do not even the publicans the same? And if ye salute your brethren only, what do ye more *than others?* Do not even the publicans so? Be ye therefore perfect, even as your Father which is in heaven is perfect."

And here again we see how the teaching of Jesus pointed them to another sublime and wonderful truth, what their theology did not seem to have embraced, the great doctrine of the universal benevolence of God; harmonizing with his works, in the outward creation, where he hath opened his hand and supplieth the wants of every living creature, "and maketh his sun to shine on the evil and on the good, and causeth his rain to descend on the just and on the unjust."

It is the crowning glory of the Christian religion, that it brings into view the infinite benevolence of the Deity; disarms him of those frailties and passions that belong only to man, and presents him to us, not in the light of a God of hatred and wrath and war, but a being of infinite perfection, purity and love. It was, therefore, a beautiful illustration of his attributes, which Jesus gave when he was enforcing the practice of those doctrines which would bring man into communion with his Maker.

Now, I cannot believe that Christianity requires less of us in the present day than it did when the blessed Jesus uttered these precepts. It is not a changeable and fluctuating religion—the kingdom of heaven is inaccessible now, as ever it has been, except by the door of obedience to Christ. "If any man will be my disciple, he must deny self, and take up his daily cross and follow me."

How appropriate was this language of Jesus to the Jews. They were so full of their traditions, so devoted to their religious notions and opinions, and so attached to their outward rituals, their sacrifices and offerings, that he said to them, ye must "leave all and follow me;" that their religion might not stand in their ceremonial worship, but in obedience to these great principles of truth, which would lead into works of righteousness.

This language is also applicable to us. Our profession of religion will be in vain if we do not become acquainted with these first principles of the gospel of Christ, and regulate our lives and conduct by them; and, we all do know what is required of us —we all may become followers of Christ, and the children of our Father in heaven.

Let us, then, take such a view of the religion of Jesus Christ, as will prompt us to the fulfilment of duty, and urge us onward in the pursuit of those riches "which moth and rust shall not corrupt, nor thieves break through and steal." Keep continually in view, that the great aim of the gospel, is to pronounce upon us the blessings of heaven—"Blessed are the meek, for they shall inherit the earth; blessed are the merciful, for they shall obtain mercy; blessed are the pure in heart, for they shall see God; blessed are they that mourn, for they shall be comforted; blessed are the peace-makers, for they shall be called the children of God."

As we are engaged in carrying out, in the daily practice of life, this high profession of Christianity, we shall find the truth of these sayings of Jesus confirmed by our own experience; by being faithful in the little, we shall be made rulers of more; we shall find that the "path of the just shineth brighter and brighter unto the perfect day," so that the nearer we approach the solemn termination of the present life, the clearer will be our views of the immortality of the soul, and the high enjoyment that is connected with the society of angelic spirits in the world to come. And while we are passing along through this present state of probation, let not our minds be so absorbed and occupied with the things that pertain only to this life, as to leave unexamined those great truths that bear such an important relation to our present and future well-being. There are riches that "moth and rust doth not corrupt, nor thieves break through and steal." These should be made the chief object of our pursuits. It is not enough that our admiration is excited in the contemplation of the goodness of God, as manifested in his outward creation. If he maketh his sun to shine on the good and evil, and causeth his rain to descend on the just and unjust, it is to teach us that benevolence is displayed in his works, and if we would be like him it must also be manifest in ours. The outward creation with all its beauties not only convinces us that it is the production of infinite power and skill, but that ample provision has been made for the happiness of man while passing through this present probationary scene. All the intellectual gifts which our Creator has bestowed, find room for employment in a plan of creation so wisely arranged, and so wonderfully diversified. In the rational exercise of these gifts we may trace out and admire the operations of Deity in the natural world, and by continued obedience to the "manifestation of the Spirit, given to every man to profit withal," enjoy union and communion with him here and for ever. It is through the exercise of spiritual gifts already bestowed upon us, that we shall become "heirs of God and joint heirs with Christ." And it seems to me that the culture and right application of these, must ever be attended with the highest degree of enjoyment for an intelligent being, and crowned with the greatest good of which we can ever partake. If these are rightly improved, we become worshippers of God in spirit and in truth. I am aware, however, that the views of worship which many entertain lead them to ceremonial acts of devotion—outward forms, divers washings, and a variety of external observances are combined to form what men have called systems of worship, in which it is presumed that assemblies of people can join and thereby bring glory to God. But it should be remembered, that as the attributes of Deity are infinite and perfect, there can be nothing added to their glory by any external act of ours. True worship is *obedience to his will.* And there is no value in any form or in any ceremony unless the heart is made better—God's blessing rests on the "pure in heart, the meek, the merciful, the peace-makes." It is with these that He owns an eternal fellowship.

If the outward law given to the Jews, with all its external ceremonies—its temples, its priests, its altars and sacrifices, could not, as Paul declares—"make those who did the service perfect, as pertaining to the conscience," or was not adequate "to take away sin," how can we expect that any outward observances, or profession of religion, can make us perfect, or so far redeem us from sin as to bring us into union with God? But if we know an inward purification of heart—a sin subdued—any turbulent passion conquered, or a victory obtained over the "lust of the flesh, the lust of the eye, and the pride of life," then indeed have we approached nearer to the Father of spirits, and our worship becomes useful to us and acceptable to him. Let us, then, seek first the "kingdom of heaven," and fulfil the "righteousness thereof," and all things pertaining to our present and future well-being will be added unto us. We shall find that in the kingdom of heaven there is perfect discipline and order; the whole mind becomes subject to the law and cross of Christ. The discipline and exercise of the mind which is then established, leads us to cease to do evil, and try to do well; to cultivate the fruits of the spirit; love peace, meekness, gentleness, mercy, charity—these are among the trees of the garden of Eden, so beautifully mentioned in the figurative language of the Scriptures, which man was commanded to dress and to keep, and of the fruit of which he might freely partake and live. My brother or my sister, consult thy own experience, and know that the spirit of truth, which is calling thee into this kingdom, where the truth only reigns, is nothing short of a ray of Divine light, emanating from the Infinite Mind—the sun of righteousness—for the blessed purpose of enlightening thy pathway and instructing thy understanding in the way in which thou should go. Obey its voice and thy soul shall live. It shows to thee with as much clearness as ever the light of the sun in the outward firmament has enabled thee to behold visible things, that the reward of obedience is peace and joy, and the consequence of transgression, remorse and anguish of spirit.

While Christianity unfolds to our view the universal benevolence of our Father in heaven, and pronounces the blessing upon the meek, the merciful, the pure in heart, the peace-makers; it also banishes from the minds of men those views of the origin of evil which have so much annoyed the happiness of the human family, and which are still embodied in many of the systems of religious belief to which the people are called.

I know that it is asserted by many, that in consequence of the transgression of our first parents, we are all sinners in the Divine sight; and they cling to the doctrine of human depravity with as much tenacity as they entertain a hope for the salvation of the soul. These baneful influences are ascribed to the temptation of some great evil spirit, separate and distinct from man, whose business, according to their creed, seems to be, to overthrow the kingdom of heaven, and defeat the benevolent purposes of God. If such a being exist, whence had he an origin? and by whom was he endowed with such great power? He could not have been created, for all that God made was good; or, if originally created good, he fell by transgression, and became the enemy of the Creator, it is a terrible delusion to suppose that he would be clothed with the powers that are ascribed to him as a reward for his wickedness. If self-existent, then there is more than one eternal Being.

But, whence cometh evil, and where hath sin its origin? The Apostle James hath illustrated this subject in a very plain manner—"Let no man say when he is tempted, I am tempted of God, for God cannot be tempted with evil, neither tempteth he any man. But every man is tempted when he is drawn away of his *own lust* and enticed; for lust, when it is conceived, bringeth forth sin, and sin when it is finished, bringeth forth death." Here we see that the origin of evil in us, is not the result of any human depravity over which we have no control, but begins when we yield to any temptation, or indulgence, which we know to be inconsistent with the Divine will.

Jesus never taught the doctrine of original depravity. His language, "Suffer little children to come unto me, and forbid them not, for of such is the kingdom of heaven," is too plain to admit of but the one meaning. It confirms the testimony of Scripture, which says, "The son shall not bear the iniquity of the father, neither shall the father bear the iniquity of the son." And again; "Thou hast been in Eden, the garden of God; every precious stone was thy covering, thou was perfect in all thy ways, from the day in which thou wast created, till iniquity was found in thee."

The pure and heavenly doctrines of Jesus, show us that the author of our being is a God of love; that justice and mercy and truth are his attributes, and that he is continually disposed to bless his dependent children. He has planned the universe for the enjoyment of his creatures, and created intelligent man, with a view to his happiness here and for ever. This notion of original sin is inconsistent with the attributes of justice and mercy which belong to the Deity; and a more irrational and absurd opinion cannot be promulgated, than that which ascribes our temptations and sins to the influence of such a being possessing the power to oppose the will of God, and perpetually to torment his rational creation. This great imaginary devil, which a gloomy theology has employed to frighten people into religion, through fear of the terrible torments he has power to inflict in the world to come, is cast out by the gospel, and we are taught, that our greatest enemies are those of our own house. Instead of looking without us for an imaginary tempter or evil spirit, we should watch over our own thoughts, actions, tempers and dispositions, lest they gain the ascendency over our better feelings, and make us the servants of sin. Instead of being driven into religion through fear, we should seek righteousness for righteousness' sake; we should love God because he is lovely; we should imitate and practice the virtues of Christ, because they lead to permanent and eternal peace.

These views have been presented to my mind, and I have offered them for our examination. Let us not be so attached to preconceived opinions, to theories or systems of faith, to creeds or speculations of men, as to be unwilling to examine them and judge for ourselves. Remember that the truth cannot be injured by the most rigid investigation, and whatever fails to stand this test is unworthy of our regard. My young friends, these are subjects that concern you, and I ask you to enter the field of inquiry in search of truth; the temptations of the future will test the strength of your allegiance to virtue; you will need a guide to direct your steps; examine into the nature of the gospel as it is revealed to your own minds, and it will direct you in the way in which you should go. If that gospel requires you to forsake the sin that doth so easily beset you, to make a sacrifice of any selfish spirit, disposition, or temper, it is because the indulgence of these things will be your ruin, and whatever delight you may take in them now, the end will prove to be "vanity and vexation of spirit." If it requires you to love your enemies; to do good to them that hate you, and pray for them that despitefully use you; bear in mind that it designs thereby to make you the children of our Father in heaven; if it asks you to be meek, to be merciful, to be pure in heart, to be peace-makers, it is, that you may enjoy all the blessings that emanate from God, the infinite fountain of all good, and extend throughout his spiritual creation, uniting his children together here by ties that death cannot sever, and preparing them for the society of the just made perfect, when these outward temples shall moulder in the dust, and the spirit return to the bosom of its Author.

THE END.

www.ingramcontent.com/pod-product-compliance
Lightning Source LLC
LaVergne TN
LVHW021423110826
845150LV00007B/2063